The Fat of the Land

by John Seymour

SELF-SUFFICIENCY: The Science and Art
of Producing and Preserving your
own Food
(with Sally Seymour)

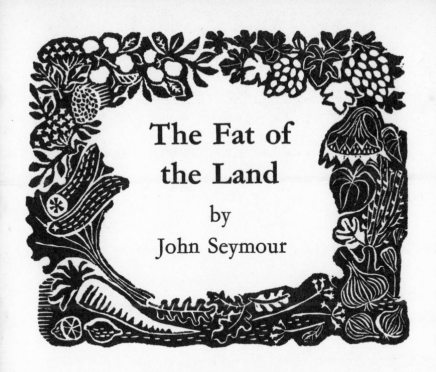

The Fat of the Land

by
John Seymour

WITH ILLUSTRATIONS BY
SALLY SEYMOUR

FABER AND FABER
3 Queen Square
London

First published in 1961
by Faber and Faber Limited
3 Queen Square London WC1
First published in this edition 1974
Reprinted 1974
Printed in Great Britain by
Unwin Brothers Limited, Old Woking, Surrey
All rights reserved

ISBN 0 571 10532 7

Contents

———

1. WE SWALLOW THE ANCHOR   *page* 9

2. WE ARE NOT VEGETARIANS   21

3. WE GET A COW   34

4. THE VEGETABLE KINGDOM   48

5. BACK TO THE HOUSE   59

6. PIGS   73

7. THE LAND   85

8. TO PRESERVE WHAT WE PRODUCE   99

9. THE RAFT-LOADS   114

10. WILD FOOD   125

11. THE HORSE   132

12. UP TO NOW   141

13. OUR FOREIGN TRADE   154

14. THIRTEEN YEARS AFTER   163

    INDEX   175

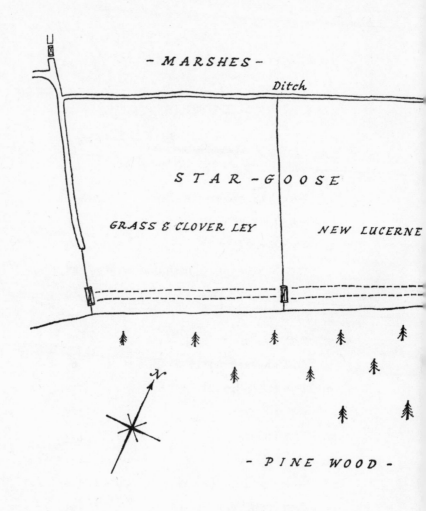

- MARSHES -

Ditch

STAR - GOOSE

GRASS & CLOVER LEY   NEW LUCERNE

N

- PINE WOOD -

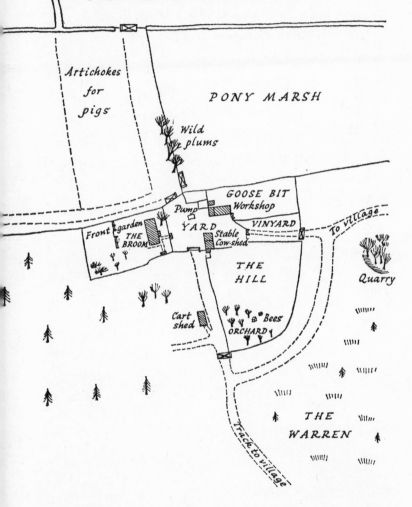

BOB WARD'S CARR MARSH

Artichokes
for
pigs

PONY MARSH

Wild
plums

GOOSE BIT

Pump   Workshop

Front garden   YARD   VINYARD

THE
BROOM   Stable
Cow-shed

To village

THE
HILL

Quarry

Cart
shed   Bees

ORCHARD

THE
WARREN

Track to village

The author would like to express his appreciation
of the valuable criticism which Mr. Lawrence D. Hills
gave to the manuscript of this book

I

We Swallow the Anchor

$\cdot$———————$\cdot$

The other day I found myself wondering just how it had come to pass that my wife and I, and our three small daughters (the smallest only a week old as I write this), should be living in the highly civilized county of Suffolk very much as if we had been cast up on a desert island.

Here we all sit, Sally my wife, Jane who is five and a half, Ann who is two and a half, and Kate who is seven (days), a mile from a hard road, with no electricity, no gas, no deliveries of anything at all excepting coal, provided that we take at least a ton, and mail, and the post woman gets specially paid for coming here. And we are self-supporting for every kind of food excepting tea, coffee, flour, sugar and salt. We have no car—we drive about with a pony and cart.

If the rest of the world blew itself up tomorrow we could go on living quite happily here and hardly notice the difference. We could (and probably soon will anyway) produce our own flour, honey could (and if I can overcome my natural repugnance to the inhabitants of the two bee hives that we have soon will) take the place of sugar. Salt we could get by evaporating sea water on a nearby beach over a drift-wood fire. Tea and coffee we could no doubt learn to do without. And there are one or two herbal teas possible—I should imagine pretty revolting they are too.

True, although Sally does "run up" almost all of her own and the children's clothes, and my shirts (and there have been ominous rumours of trousers and a jacket) we do not yet make

9

our own cloth. But in a mad moment we bought a big table loom (it was going for a song), and this autumn are probably getting some in-lamb ewes as an experiment. And I notice some gruesome bundles of alum-dressed rabbit skins in a cupboard. Indeed it would be hard for anybody who had not got a bad cold not to notice them. I can foresee the day when I shall be sent out into the world looking like a cross between Davy Crockett and Robinson Crusoe. Nothing would surprise me.

We never meant to go like this. Or at least I didn't. With Sally you can never tell.

We were a fairly ordinary couple when we married. True, I lived aboard a Dutch sailing smack (often miscalled a "barge") and Sally lived in Hammersmith and made her living by making pots down in the basement. She had an electric kiln there, and froze when it was off and roasted when it was on. She once put a bottle of red wine in it—to *chambre* it quickly (a brutal thing to do anyway) and the cork blew out and the wine ruined a whole kiln-full of pots.

As for me I lived aboard this sailing boat (when I say that she was a sailing smack—she was built on the lines of one but as a yacht), moored up at such places as Richmond, Chelsea, Upnor which is a small village near Rochester on the Medway, Pin Mill which is a small village up the Orwell in Suffolk, and anywhere else that took my fancy. I could live this nomadic life because I could earn my living (which was a very modest one it is true) by writing for the B.B.C. and also occasionally bolting off to India or Africa and writing a travel book.

When we got married Sally settled down happily enough aboard the *Jenny the Third*, and we continued, for a year or two, the old, pleasant, rather rootless, nomadic life. In fact we intensified it; for we sailed along the east coast of England, into the Wash and its rivers, into the Trent, up to Nottingham, down to the Humber, up the Yorkshire Ouse to Ripon, then across the Penine chain along the Leeds-Liverpool Canal, back again to Suffolk, and finally across to Holland where we poked about among the waterways there.

Now this aquatic wandering would have suited me for the

rest of my life. I had plans of sailing up the Rhine and down the Danube (everyone who has ever floated on a horse-pond in a tin bath has had *that* dream), "doing" the "Med", the Red Sea, across to Ceylon (which I looked upon in those days as my second home), then maybe Indonesia where the girls are so pretty and wear so few clothes. And all that.

But little Jane grew older, and began to crawl about the saloon floor under my feet. Whenever we were caught in a breeze of wind and I would shout for Sally to come and take the wheel while I triced up the tack of the mainsail (you get lazy about reefing in a Dutchman) she would come up with a baby under one arm which reduced her efficiency as a sailor. She never said much—but I could see that she craved to make pots again. She had been a good potter—one of the best decorators of ceramics in London—and it seemed a shame that her talents should be sacrificed on the altar of my wanderlust. We both wanted more children, and the idea of yet *more* babies crawling about on that saloon carpet frightened me. And we both, I suppose, had the home-making urge.

So we decided to sell the boat and buy a house.

Now Sally had been brought up in Australia, and one part of England was as good as another to her. So it was left to me to choose a place. I chose Suffolk. My home had been in North Essex but Essex, alas, has become one sprawling suburb. Norfolk is fine—but too near the Midlands. It is gradually being colonized from there as Essex has been colonized from London. Suffolk is in between. Besides I knew Suffolk. Somewhere in East Anglia it had to be, because I like East Anglians. I talk the lingo.

I took Sally down to the Oyster Inn at the tiny village of Butley, and she sat there all evening terrified lest someone should address some remark to her—because she couldn't understand anything anybody said!

Now an unfortunate thing had happened when we were wintering, in the early part of 1956, at the summit of the Leeds-Liverpool Canal.

There we were, at an altitude of five hundred feet, with

Jenny lying on the canal and ourselves living, temporarily, in an old stone farm cottage that a farmer had lent to us for the winter. The snow came, the canal froze up nearly solid, *Jenny* was locked in an icy grip, and I had forgotten to turn the sea cock of the lavatory system off. Curse all patent lavatory systems in small boats—what is wrong with a bucket? A thaw came, and we looked out of the window one morning to find *Jenny* sunk. The cold had broken the lavatory pipe and *Jenny*—which had weathered gales on the North Sea and the English Channel—was sitting on the muddy bottom of the Leeds-Liverpool Canal.

We spent a couple of days pumping her out, with motor-driven pumps borrowed from farmers. Eventually we managed to raise her. But the water had got into her engine jacket and frozen in there and bust that too. About five hundred books had to be carted away by the dust cart. Etcetera, etcetera. The insurance company, with a bit of prodding, turned out fairly handsome; but the upshot of it was that *Jenny* was towed away down the cut to—of all places in the world for a sea-going sailing vessel to find herself—Bradford, where she had to undergo extensive repairs.

Meanwhile, Sally and I bought an old car and travelled to the south of England again. We were homeless, and so our house-hunting urge was precipitated. An old friend, who had a farm just north of Ipswich, very kindly allowed us to live in a deserted wing of his tudor farmhouse, while we searched for a house of our own.

The wing of the farmhouse was unfurnished; but we had some heavy old Yorkshire farmhouse furniture which a very kind cattle dealer had lent us to put in our stone cottage by the banks of the Leeds-Liverpool Canal. When we had offered to return it he had refused, saying that he had furnished his house out with modern stuff (all veneer and streamlined curves—I never could see why a sideboard has to be streamlined—it is not expected to fly through the air) and we were welcome to it. So we had it shipped down from the north, and there we were in our wing of the farmhouse, with a couple of colossal walnut sideboards, some packing-cases to sit on, an old kitchen table to eat off, a mattress on the floor to sleep on, and for me I would have been happy to have gone on like that for the rest of my life. And we had the little calor-gas stove out of the boat.

Then started this house-hunt, and this took us the whole summer.

What made this house hunt so very difficult was the fact that —although we wanted a very good house—we did not have any money. We had so little money—or rather we had such a large *minus quantity* of money—that we calculated that even after we had sold *Jenny the Third* we would still not have any money. And yet there we were having our names put down on the list of every house-agent in East Suffolk, and travelling around the countryside in our old car looking at endless houses.

And anyway we did not see one that we liked.

Here again there was a difficulty: we did not know what we wanted.

Certainly we did not want a farm. Sally is a potter—I am a writer. We are not farmers, and did not want to be cluttered up with a farm. The fact that we did not have two brass halfpennies to rub together was not the fact which dissuaded us from getting a farm. A modern house would not do: because all modern houses which are for sale in East Suffolk (we found) are ugly. We could not live in an ugly and badly proportioned house. We wanted a very large garden and perhaps a field or two. We thought we might like to keep a horse. We had to have enough room for Sally's pottery, and also enough room to put up the large number of friends which we knew would invade us. We were quite used to having fifteen people sleeping aboard *Jenny*. There had to be room for drunken parties, song and argument, and sleeping children, in the same house. We would not live on a main road (we are not mad), we would not live just dumped down in a field anywhere. There had to be a *reason* for the choice of a site for whatever house we lived in. We would not live near a town. We would not live bang in a village. (I think we might have been wrong there. There is something nice about village life.)

We Swallow the Anchor

I suppose we must have gone and looked at perhaps fifty houses and cottages.

Finally we decided: we would have to build our own house.

We found a perfect site: in the parish of Holbrook, overlooking the estuary of the River Stour.

A field of a couple of acres, with a tall hedge around it, running right down to the edge of the estuary, approached by a farm track, on a south-facing slope. We would buy that, build a house on it, and the house would have the grandest view in East Anglia across the mile-wide Stour. We would buy up old sailing barges, break the timbers out of them, build a timber-framed building and fill the interstices in with planking lined with hardboard, or perhaps the traditional wattle and daub. Why not? What our ancestors could do we could do too. We would build one room at first and then gradually add to it. We would do this with our own hands, while at the same time earning a living writing and potting, digging the two acres and planting things on it, producing a lot of our own food, and in our spare time fishing and wild-fowling on the River Stour. The man *nearly* sold us the field: and then thought better of it. The last time I went there I found a large modern house (I must say not a badly proportioned one) built just where we had wanted to have ours. But built by a proper builder, for somebody who evidently had plenty of brass.

Then we got a letter from a man who owned an estate near another estuary—much farther north.

We had forgotten all about that.

For, after we had been searching for about a couple of months, we had struck on the idea of writing to a number of owners of big estates asking them if they had any old empty cottages, either to sell or to rent.

In our travels about the country, we had found that in every parish, as soon as we got off the road, there were empty cottages. Old gamekeepers' cottages, or old farm workers' cottages. The gamekeepers had gone off to jobs more in keeping with the people's democracy, the farm workers to be planted out in council houses, nicely spaced, like spring cabbages in the autumn. For how could their wives live without electric light and the *pukey*, which I understand is the latest name for the goggle-box? So this country of England is covered with fine little cottages, and big ones too, and also farm houses, which are empty, and either derelict or soon will be.

But it is not easy to buy or rent one of these empty houses. Most of the owners just do not want them lived in. They would rather they fell down in fact. People are always a bit of a nuisance to big landowners. Such people as are still necessary to drive the combine harvesters and hang on the milking machines are best housed in council houses where they are out of the way, and are not allowed to keep dogs. We had asked many an owner about many an empty cottage, and had always been met with refusal. Since then many of these cottages have fallen down.

But here was a letter from a very nice man saying—yes—he had an empty cottage—two in fact stuck together, but so remote that he did not think that anybody would want to live in them. But still—we could go and look at them. If we liked the look of them we could rent them for a purely nominal rent— with a bit of land. Simply because they were nice-looking cottages and he did not wish to see them fall down.

Remote!

Remote they were indeed. We drove over to meet the land-owner, who proved to be a young, very tall, very public school, man named Michael. He put us in his Landrover and drove us away from the village which was remote enough in itself, being twelve miles from the nearest town—twelve miles mostly of forestry plantations owned by the Forestry Commission. Miles and miles of pine forest.

And here we were, being bounced along a farm track, in this desperate Landrover, across fields of light land, across heath land, through bracken, until we wondered just where he was taking us.

Then—when we seemed to be miles away from anywhere (which indeed we were) we saw the back of a double cottage. It stood with a pine wood the other side of it, a big area of bracken-covered hillside on one side of it and a great area of marshland the other. We could see at first just a big expanse of mossy thatch, for there—at the back of the house—the steep thatched roof comes within seven feet of the ground.

We stopped at a gate. There was a collection of outbuildings behind the house. There was a rough three-acre field beside it. All grown up with weeds and thistles. There were nettles everywhere in the gardens of the two cottages, and in the yard behind. Nettles, brambles, thistles, weeds were the key-note. One at least had an impression of fertility. If weeds will grow so will anything else.

One approached the two cottages from behind—for in front of them were their fenced-in front gardens, big by town standards, enclosed on two sides by the pine plantation, fenced from the three-acre field on the other.

One of the cottages was occupied.

It was all a bit of a tragedy.

The two cottages had always been occupied—by game-keepers or stockmen, until after the war when one—the right-hand one—became empty and stayed empty. The left-hand one was still occupied, however, by a man and his wife, the man was a stockman working for the owner. His wife had been born in the cottage, and had spent all of her life there. Then, she had been stricken with arthritis and completely crippled. In her early forties she had been deprived of her legs, and the use of her hands, until she had become nothing but a mind—and a spirit—inhabiting the useless remains of a body. The man had left his employment with the landlord, owing to reasons which have got nothing to do with me, and had got a job on "The Island"—a Government establishment not involved in farming—where most people work round here.

So here was this poor bed-ridden woman, cared for tenderly and faithfully by her over-driven husband, both before he left to cycle off to his bread-winning in the morning, and after he got back at night, or by the district nurse who had to make that bumpy and difficult drive every day to go and minister to her.

Now if she had been an ordinary woman this would not have been so terrible. But Janet is an outstanding woman. She had spent her life in that remote place, reared her family there, and grown into it. She knew, and loved, every bird, every flower, every plant, every tree, every weed. Still, when I go and see her as I do all too seldom, she will sit propped up on her pillow and her eyes light up as she tells me to look in a certain place along the hedge and see if the tiger lilies she planted there years ago are in bloom, or does that little bunch of daffodils she put up among the bracken on the hill where her husband kept his bees still come up in the spring? Very few country women now-adays would live at the Broom. Janet is one of the few who would—and would love it.

But these people were leaving. A council house had been got for them. Janet would be taken away almost by force, for even if she was bed-ridden she loved the Broom. But it was not fair that the district nurse should have that journey every day, nor that her husband should go on for ever doing two days' work every twenty-four hours.

Meanwhile, Ken could hardly have been expected to keep the garden even on his side in good order. He was nurse, cook, cleaner and bottle washer before and after his work. He could hardly be gardener too. He kept a goat, for the milk, grew a few rose bushes because *she* loved them, and that was that.

Anyway, Michael took us into the empty side of the house, and we looked around.

A lean-to kitchen on the back, dark, tile-floored, with a copper and a little old-fashioned coal range in it. A fair-sized pantry giving off it. A door into the room in which I sit now—a squarish room with a low ceiling supported by a single oak beam (the room is eighteen by fifteen feet). This had an ordinary small open fireplace and a rough brick floor. Giving off this two more rooms, which had obviously been added at a later date—small rooms which had probably been extra bedrooms. Then, up the very narrow and winding stairway, two very small bedrooms. Excepting for the two added bedrooms down-stairs the other cottage was the same as this, we were told, but it had had a lavatory and a bathroom added on to it as well.

The windows in front of the cottages were pointed, in the Gothic style. One imagined that they had been put in about a hundred and fifty years ago. But the house might have been much older: in fact there is a tradition that "there has always been a house down at the Broom". Indeed as I dig in the garden I find medieval hand-wrought nails, old tiles, and queer-sized bricks, some without frogs. The Romans had a camp near here. There are chipped flints about.

From the upper windows—which faced the front—south-west—the view was blocked on two sides by the pine wood; but to the west there was a fine open vista—across the marshes, with a river wall and then low hills (*very* low—after all this is Suffolk) beyond. Marshes into which woods intrude, and on which stands—or stood—an old windmill, the purpose of which was to pump the water out of the marshes into the estuary over the wall. The windmill blew down in a gale the year before last.

The view was not spectacular, by any means. The pine wood was a bit gloomy. The house was not "a gem". The style— "estate gothic"—was not our favourite. The addition of the two little rooms at one end gave the building a queer, lopsided look. The thatch came down only a few feet in front but nearly to the ground on that side. In the winter, obviously, the pine wood would very much cut off the sun.

"I'll let you have the two cottages, the out-houses, the field, in all about five acres, for ten pounds a year—provided that you keep it in repair," said Michael.

"You're on," I said. And Sally agreed with me.

We looked at the outhouses. There was a long, well-built, brick building with a tiled roof which had once been used for rearing pheasants. It had a little room at one end of it with a fireplace in over which the mash for the little victims had once been cooked. This, we decided, would make a food store, and the main part of the building Sally's pottery. There was a weather-board building which had once been a stable and cow-shed. There was a piece of land—the segment of a circle—be-hind the house, covered with high bracken but fenced in from the bracken-covered hillside beyond by a rabbit-proof wire fence. As this sloped upwards we called it "The Hill". Michael's father, before he died, let the Forestry Commission have the land beyond the fence on a ninety-nine year lease for an old song to plant their everlasting pines on. Then there was a big fenced patch which had once been two vegetable gardens, in the days when men still had the guts and the energy to grow their own food. This was by the time we saw it but a wired-in enclosure head-high with nettles and tall weeds. So overgrown was it that we could not even see that there was an old shep-herd's wheeled hut down at the end of it which had once served as a pigsty.

So there it was.

"It's ours," we said, and drove back to our temporary quarters, and thereupon started a long-drawn-out series of negotiations with some firm of lawyers in Leeds of all places. And, in due course, a contract was made out. The Broom was ours, on a twenty-five year lease, for a rent—(not of ten pounds a year it is true for the lawyers were not so generous as Michael) but of twenty-five pounds a year plus rates. The rates were very small.

Our house-hunt was at an end.

But we still had no idea of ever becoming a kind of twentieth-century Swiss Family Robinson. We merely wanted somewhere pleasant to live, that we could afford. And we had found it.

2

We ate not Vegetarians

We could not move into the Broom immediately, for
various reasons. For one thing: until the contract
was signed our landlord did not wish us to move in.
If we had done so, I suppose, and the contract had not been
agreed to by either side, it might have been hell's own business
getting us out again. For another—we had to fetch *Jenny the
Third* down from the north of England. You can hardly leave
a sea-going sailing vessel for ever in a place like Bradford.
Then we had to sell her. And also, before we sold her, we had
to sail her to Holland and back.

We had decided that we wanted to make one last cruise in her
before moving ashore for good.

Having recently got a little money for writing a book we
were able to sell the old car (which was falling to pieces—as all
second-hand cars do immediately I start to own them) and buy
a new Bedford Dormobile. We were hustled into doing this for
several reasons. One was that a new law had just been enacted
clapping purchase tax on vans with windows at the back, and
by buying immediately we were just able to save £200. Another
was that it was evident that we would shortly wish to move a
lot of furniture about. Another was that in my work for the
B.B.C. I had to travel about the country a lot and a dormobile
was convenient because one could sleep in it. You can sleep in
Grosvenor Square in a dormobile, and nobody knows you're
there until you've gone.

Into this we stuffed such furniture as we had acquired by

various means (we had been going to a lot of sales, and junk shops) and carried it over, a load at a time, to the Broom, where we piled it in the one big room on the empty side of the house. We also started digging the front garden.

We bought some tools, slashed down the undergrowth in the garden out at the front on the empty side of the house, pared the turf off with a mattock, and then dug it. The turf we piled up at one side of the cottage to make "compost" and it is still there—a man-made small mountain covered with nettles and spear grass (couch grass)—and as far as I can see it always will be there.

We knew nothing at all about gardening but we bought a book on it. Also Ken, our neighbour, would look through the hedge sometimes and give us advice. We bought a lot of Brassica plants—brussels sprouts, broccoli, cabbages, red cabbage —and planted them, and also put in everything else we could think of. Ken told us that we would harvest nothing of this for the birds would get it all. Pigeons and pheasants. Ah, we thought. We will not be so easily beaten. And we rigged up a fantastic and complicated system of fences made with black cotton, five feet high, cutting the land up into small squares, so that any bird wishing to get into it would find himself entrapped in a network of invisible black threads such as would put him off our garden for good.

This was fine. Our crops suffered no damage from pheasants. But if the cotton fences kept the birds off—they also kept us off. To hoe the crops—standing and poking about amid all that cotton—was to be driven mad. One's hoe—one's feet—one's self would become tangled up with black cotton like a fly in a spider's web. And then we went and fetched *Jenny*, and sailed away to Holland, and forgot all about the Broom and our crops for four months. Naturally our newly dug garden was not very productive. But even so—when we finally did get back to the Broom again, there was enough green stuff among the weeds to keep us meagrely in vegetables for the rest of the winter and the "hungry gap" in the spring. So our effort was not altogether wasted.

We are not Vegetarians

We sailed back from Holland, berthed *Jenny* in a creek behind Canvey Island to be painted up and then sold, and moved into the Broom late on the freezing cold night of the nineteenth of December.

In our usual happy fashion we had not ordered any coal to be delivered, nor anything else in fact. But Michael, who at least knew we were coming, had had the kindness to take a sack of coal down there, and light a fire in the living-room. We cleared a space on the floor, dumped a mattress on it and the baby's basket (we still only had one baby then) and went to sleep.

Next day life began in earnest. And I really believe that if we could have imagined all the toil and moil and groil that stood between us then, and us *now* as I write this sentence (if it can be called a sentence) we would have picked up the baby and run screaming from the place.

Firstly, there was so much to do just to stay alive that we both simply moved about in a kind of a daze, like ants whose nest has been turned up with a spade.

In a kind of blind, desperate way we dragged furniture about, slapped whitewash about, drove over the rough tracks to the village to buy food, order coal. We intended to heat the place mostly with wood, which we could get for nothing; but thought it wouldn't be a bad idea to have a ton or two of coal

as well. A belt as well as braces as it were. For it was very cold. Then—just to exist at the Broom took up time. Water, for example, had to be pumped up from the well at the back of the house with a semi-rotary pump. To get enough water for the nappies I would have to pump fifty strokes. To bath—a hundred and fifty. I got to know that pump very well.

Our former neighbours, Ken and Janet, had gone. They were installed in their council house. Their side of the house was empty: excepting for the sense that one had of their occupation. People cannot live a lifetime in a house, and feel for it as Janet had felt for her house, and go away and leave no trace of themselves.

We only went into their side of the house when we wanted to go to the bathroom or the lavatory. Three days after we had moved in, on the shortest day of the year. I took an axe upstairs and broke through the lath and plaster wall in the bedroom cupboard to emerge unscathed in the bedroom cupboard of the other cottage.

People came for Christmas. They slept about all over the place: upstairs and downstairs and in my lady's parlour. They have been sleeping about all over the place off and on ever since. They sleep on a camp bed that we bought, on mattresses on the floor, on the mat in front of the fire: a man named Tom once tried to sleep on three chairs, but was so horribly uncomfortable that he gave it up in the middle of the night and went for a walk. A man named Arthur—tired of walking out into the garden and going round to the next cottage every time he wanted to go to the lavatory—got a hammer and a cold chisel and knocked a hole through the brick wall which separated the two kitchens. We whitewashed the kitchens, and slowly began to sort ourselves out.

While Christmas was on, and we were settling in as it were, life went on quite amusingly. But then Sally began to try to make pots, and I began to write. And then we found that the shoe began to pinch.

For every single thing we wanted we had to go a mile and a half to the village to buy it. Our milk we arranged to have left every morning at some cottages a mile away from us, and every morning somebody had to go and get this. We had perhaps vaguely talked, once or twice in our lives, of one day "keeping a cow". But this had been mere castle-building. We had never had any real intention of keeping a cow. But now we began to think very seriously of getting a cow. I had ample time, every morning, as I slogged over the warren with the empty milk bottles, and slogged back with the full ones, to think about getting a cow.

We had never had any real conscious drive to self-sufficiency. We had thought, like a lot of other people, that it would be nice to grow our own vegetables. Well—we were doing so. More or less.

Now my income depends—and it depended then—on the amount of paid work that I do. If I spend every day of my life scheming and working, and running about the country recording people, and writing things, and sending off nice letters to editors or producers, I can earn quite a lot of money. But at the Broom—all this sort of thing seemed to be less important. We began to break up more land—clear the brushwood and weeds away, dig and weed. As our gardening book told us to plant we planted. This was all very nice: but there was a spectacular drop in our income. We began to think twice about slogging into the village and paying thirty shillings for a joint of beef.

We might just as well, we thought, start producing our own meat.

We drove back to the farmer friend with whom we had been staying north of Ipswich, and bought from him half a dozen geese and about a dozen ducks. The geese were white ones, and the ducks had a lot of mallard in them. We put all these birds loose in the back of the dormobile and drove back to the Broom. One of the ducks kept roosting on my lap as I tried to drive and a goose pecked me in the ear; but we got them all home without other incident. The geese, the wings of which were clipped, we turned loose in the fenced vegetable enclosure at the back of the buildings, and ever since that day we have never called that enclosure anything else than "Goose Bit". Thus do fields and plots of land get named, and their names stay with them for always. We have taken care, since then, to find the proper names of other fields about the Broom, so that their tradition will never be altered through our ignorance. Our own three-acre field is called Star Goose. Then there are: Bob Ward's Carr (a marshy wood), Bob Ward's Carr Marsh, Whin's Marsh, Stetch Marsh, Fleet Marsh, Mill Marsh, Pony Marsh, Keeper's Walk, Skirts, Fleet Marsh, and the rest of it. These marshes were only enclosed from the sea in the Middle Ages, and probably the fields themselves were not made so many centuries ago. So these names are not ancient like the names of fields in the longer settled parfs of the country, where field names sometimes go back to Saxon times.

The geese made their way into the jungle that was "Goose Bit", and seemed to be fairly much at home.

The ducks we shut in a nettle-grown pen which was already there. Neither of us had ever kept birds before, and we felt very uncertain what to do with these animals. We found a water mill farther up our estuary, owned by a very nice farmer-miller who right from the start has been a source of good advice and strength to us, and we bought from him some mixed grain: tail wheat and barley and crushed maize. We chucked a few handfuls of this to the ducks and the geese twice a day and hoped for the best. But we felt that there must be much more to it than just this.

Acting on advice we rather fearfully let the birds out. The geese flapped their wings and screamed and tried to taxi fast enough to take off and made straight for the marshes. They put half a mile between us and them in a minute or so. The ducks just waddled away, down to the nearest ditch, and launched themselves into it.

But they all came back again. As soon as it was meal-time back they came, and we put them in their enclosures again, and let them out again in the morning.

And lo—they began to lay us eggs. The geese occasionally: the ducks every day. We soon found that the ducks laid their eggs fairly late in the morning; and therefore we learned not to let them out until about ten o'clock. They dumped their eggs just anywhere, quacked a bit, and waddled off down to the ditch to eat waterweed.

The thing to do now, we realized, was to set some eggs. We had a neighbour (if you can call a man who lived a mile and a half away over very rough country a neighbour) who was a poultry farmer, and from him we bought a Light Sussex hen which had gone broody. We put a setting of duck eggs under her. We had made an elaborate series of four hen coops (which we called "the council houses") and in Number One we put her. We named her "Henrietta", and she settled in on those eggs without a bit of trouble, and she is still with us, and still brings off at least two broods of something or other a year, and still lays us eggs, and she is sacrosanct. She would be the last in a famine to go into the boiling-pot—and then she would not go. We would starve first.

A few days later we got another broody hen (our neighbour would sell them to us for ten shillings each—he was glad to get rid of them—broodies were a nuisance to him), and we set her on some more duck eggs. We set some more on goose eggs, and some of the geese began to sit on their own eggs. One old fool made a beautiful nest right down on the edge of a ditch in Bob Ward's Carr—sat like a statue until a day before they should have hatched—and then the rain came and washed the whole boiling into the water so that was that.

Geese make fine mothers. Domestic ducks are useless.* If one kept geese commercially one would try not to let them go

* But see note on page 33 at end of chapter.

broody and sit, but keep them just as egg-laying machines, and put the eggs under hens to hatch. That first year we hatched off a lot of geese, and the rats ate some, and others had other various accidents, but we succeeded in fatting off for the winter and Christmas eighteen. Eighteen is too many geese. Actually they were useful that year, because Sally had another baby, and we found that we wanted to repay the midwife, and the doctor, and the postwoman who kindly came and cleaned the house for us when it got in a beggar's muddle, our landlord, and all the other people, male and female, who had helped us in various ways, and we were able to give them each a goose for Christmas. I suppose we could have sold geese too: but we never did. We never sell anything that we produce here, excepting Sally's pots and my writing, and the occasional calf.

For this we discovered early. Once you start trying to sell the produce of the land you enter a world of thieves and rogues and bounders in which you just cannot breathe. I know people who sell lettuces at a farthing when lettuces are selling in the shops —days old and stale and weary—at tenpence. We wish to be included out of that world, please.

But to get back to our geese. There are few things nicer to eat than a fat goose—but also there are few things more troublesome to pluck. So we found that we had to ration ourselves as to geese. There just was not time to eat too many of them. The plucking took too long. Later, we found that it was quite unnecessary to keep so many geese.

True they live on practically nothing. If you can let them wander away over the marshes, as we can, until the ten days of their lives during which you want to fatten them, they live on nothing. That is—if grass is nothing, which of course it isn't. And then there is that half-handful of corn with which you lure them home every night. But you just do not need half a dozen breeding geese. We now have three: two geese and a gander: and their increase. We do not trouble much about setting eggs, or rearing small geese. We may set one hen on goose eggs, and then we let the geese sit on their own, if they will. They can please themselves. We don't break our necks looking after them. This year we have given a couple of goslings away, we have six coming on nicely to fatten for ourselves, and the three old breeding ones, and that is that. Six fat geese is enough for a family through the year, in the goose line.

As for the ducks: they were always a success. From the beginning of February right through until midsummer they lay far more eggs than we can eat. Nothing ever goes wrong with them, we feed them very little, they are no trouble at all. Last year we bought a Khaki Campbell drake, and now have a new generation coming along: a cross between this gentleman and the old half-wild ones. They will no doubt lay even more eggs, and should, if we feed them better, lay right through the year. People say to us sometimes: "Why do you have cross breeds and mixed-up strains in your animals and poultry? It's as cheap to feed a good animal as a bad." The answer to this is that a pure-bred animal is not necessarily "better" than a mongrel. For our purposes it is generally worse. It is probably too specialized. If it has been bred to lay eggs: it will lay too many eggs, and get sick and die. If it has been bred to give milk: it will give too much milk. And cost too much to feed, and have to be molly-coddled, and have to have a vet in almost constant attendance as do commercial herds of British Friesians. For us —the all-round animal, not too highly specialized, not too developed away from the wild creature, not too finicky and highly-strung, not too productive.

Duck eggs, incidentally, are perfectly "safe"—provided that you do not cart them around and expose them to all sorts of contamination. Eaten fresh from one's own ducks they are fine.

So the ducks and geese settled down, and were not too much trouble, and provided us with eggs and with a certain amount of meat. And, as we bought broody after broody from our neighbour, all Light Sussex hens, we found that our hen flock began to increase. Somebody gave us an Indian Game cockerel. And when the broodies had hatched out and reared their broods of ducks or geese that we had given them—they began to lay eggs themselves. We never bothered about them—excepting that they came in for their share of the few handfuls of grain that we chucked the ducks and geese every day. They slept in the elder tree in the yard, and ranged far and wide every day in the wood, and scratched up earwigs and wood lice, and seemed to thrive. I do not suppose we found half the eggs that they laid—but Sally became very good at rushing out every time she heard a hen cackle and locating the patch of impenetrable nettles where her nest was. And we got enough eggs to eat (as many as we wanted—and, although they didn't have comic little lions printed on them they were at least never more than a day old) and we "put down" a lot in water-glass.

One day Henrietta came clucking back from the wood with a dozen little yellow chicks at her heels. We had discovered the secret of rearing poultry. Simply leave them absolutely and entirely alone.

I am often amazed when I see the complicated apparatus that is made, and sold for enormous sums, for hatching eggs and rearing chicks. For all you need is a *hen*. Leave the hen alone—let her go off alone in a wood and—provided that she has been introduced to a cockerel at some time—she will come waddling back in due course with a dozen little chicks. That is our experience. Nobody knows so much about rearing chicks as a hen. And the chicks that she rears will be much stronger and healthier than the poor little orphans that come out of a machine. Our miller friend once tried to sell me some chick crumbs which had been indoctrinated with some substance to immunize chicks against some disease called coccidiosis. We are simply not interested in diseases at the Broom. We don't get them. Our chicks drown themselves in the water trough fairly often—but what if they do? There are always plenty more.

Further to augment our meat supply—we were given by a friend two rabbits. We put them in a wire pen which we made, fed them on weeds, refuse from the garden, and a little bran, and they duly produced seven young rabbits. These grew up—we ate them one by one—and then, hungry devils that we were, we skoffed ma and pa as well. So that was the end of the rabbits. We will have to try again some day: they are delicious. But we get plenty of wild hares around here, and wild rabbits are beginning to come back, and tame rabbits are *rather* a lot of trouble to keep, unless you have older children to feed them and take an interest in them, and so we have never taken them up again.

At all events, our chickens, geese and ducks, together with the occasional wild creature (we are allowed to kill hares and pigeons of course) soon made up three-quarters of our meat supply. We began to be the butcher's worst customers.

Of course this meat was not free. We had to buy a little corn —a little barley meal for fattening. We had to do a little work. But it was *nearly* free. And after all that is something. We still have not solved the problem of growing all our own feeding stuffs for poultry. Whether we will or not I do not know. This year we have a small block of sunflowers outside the pottery window: we will at least experiment with this as a poultry food. If it is good, next year we can grow more. That first year we actually tried to grow a block of wheat: but the sparrows had the last grain. The little birds make it difficult to grow corn in small quantities, although I know it can be done because I know somebody who does it. If we *had* to feed our poultry off our five acres we would do it. One day we will: probably next year.

Having lived among vegetarian Hindus for a long time I have had many thoughts about this meat-eating business.

You can eat meat all your life, provided that you just buy it from the butcher, and never give the matter a thought. But when you have to kill an animal *yourself* before you can eat it, the matter appears in a different perspective. People come and stay with us sometimes and express horror at me when I kill an animal. "How could you do it?" I always ask them what they had for dinner the day before they came to see us, and if they say "meat", as they always have done up to now, I know that I can treat their scruples with contempt. If a vegetarian came I would have to treat *his* scruples at least with respect.

I do not like killing animals; but having decided, after a great deal of thought, that it is right to kill animals, I do it without worrying myself about it. I even manage to take a certain pride in doing it quickly and painlessly, in at least *aiming* at a professional standard in paunching and plucking and cleaning and butchering, and at doing the thing in a workmanlike manner.

To connive at the killing of animals while being too lily-livered to kill them yourself is despicable. We could not have milk here unless we bred calves, and what would we do with the surplus calves unless we sold them off the place—knowing that they would certainly go to the butcher? We could not have eggs unless we kept birds, and if we did not kill off surplus birds we would very soon be overrun. As it is we have to eat an awful lot of chickens to keep them down to reasonable limits.

I would like to see the experiment made of living on such a little piece of land as we have got without animals. I expect that health could be maintained among the humans by a vegetarian diet alone (but remember—there could be no cheese nor butter nor milk nor eggs—the production of these things would entail killing animals). I expect that the fertility of the soil could be kept up by vegetable composting and green manuring, but I am not sure. Possibly it would require much less land to feed a family of vegetarians than one of omnivorous people. It is an experiment that I should like to see tried. I am not sure that I would like to try it myself!

Note (See page 28). We have since found that ducks make good mothers if caught and penned as soon as they come in with their babies.

3

We Get a Cow

W ell, there we were, we at the Broom, and we found that if we were in for a penny we were in for a pound. For, to live there as we did at first, subsisting like everybody else on stuff bought from the shops, was extremely difficult. We had to slog up to the village for a loaf of bread. Luckily Sally could bake her own bread, and we bought a hundredweight of wholemeal flour and she started to do so. This is much easier than many people think: certainly easier than baking the everlasting cakes that most country people seem to live upon nowadays, and once you have got used to home-baked wholemeal bread it is very nasty to have to eat that shop-bought pap again. Two or three slices of our bread are a good meal in themselves, and the stuff is delicious. We are not concerned, and never have been, with the alleged fact that wholemeal bread is *healthier* than white. We just like it better, that is all.

We realized that we would have to get either a cow or a goat, or get out. That morning slog up for the milk every day would finish us. And we realized that whichever we had we would have to grow some fodder for it.

I spent much of my time digging, but it became evident to me that long before I had dug my way to the last bit of our piece of land the first bit that I had dug would be grown up with wilderness again. We had never thought of letting pigs do our digging for us in those days. Pigs, we now know, will dig far better than we can, and manure the ground at the same

time, and clear it of weeds, and go on growing themselves while they are doing so.

I asked our landlord Michael if he would send a tractor.

I spent a couple of days clearing Goose Bit—hacking down the weeds and brambles and making a great fire—and then along came the Ferguson and ploughed it all twelve inches deep.

But this was not the end of it. I then had to break it down, and this I found I had to do with a mattock. Bed by bed, as we needed the ground, I smacked it and smashed it with a mattock. This was extremely hard work, and very good for me. Also I had to fork over every inch of it for spear grass roots—spear grass is what we call couch grass in these parts. This is our worst enemy, and it will still be years before we completely overcome it.

It so happened that the book we had bought on growing vegetables was a book on *cloche* gardening, and so we naturally thought in terms of cloches. And when we saw a lot of barn cloches advertised in the local paper we went and bought sixty of them, for five shillings each.

They have their uses. But we should never have lashed out on a quantity like that.

In the first place it took us just six months to break *half* of them. I only have to *look* at a cloche for it to dissolve with a merry tinkle, and our first pair of pigs used to escape from their sty in the bottom of Goose Bit and tear round the garden with me after them breaking cloches.

In the second place—they are not really all *that* effective. Not unless you devote your life to serving them like a vestal virgin. But before the end of January we had sown the seeds of onions, celery, cauliflower, cabbage, lettuce, radishes and parsnips.

We were slavishly following our book—and more books which we began to buy. By now we have learnt that about the only things worth planting as early as February even are parsnips and shallots (although many things are better sown in the autumn). But in those days we tried everything, and we gave ourselves an enormous amount of work and very often for nothing.

The Englishman's home is supposed to be his castle; but considering that very few Englishmen even *own* their homes this saying is ridiculous. In most cases the Englishman's home is somebody *else's* castle. This is not the place to go in to a long one-sided argument about the merits or demerits of the land-lord-tenant system (I'll just say that I loath and detest it!) but that is so. And for this reason very few English cottagers ever plant fruit trees in their gardens. Why should they improve somebody else's property? And so the Broom, like most other cottages around these parts, was, when we came to it, devoid of fruit trees excepting for one old eating-apple tree, terribly neglected and overgrown with lichen, and the stumpy remains of a cooker, at the bottom of what had been Ken and Janet's front garden.

We decided at least to remedy this. After all, at least we knew that we had twenty-five years to enjoy the fruits of our planting.

We worried Michael into sending us a trailer load of stable manure, and then ordered a batch of two and three-year-old trees, mostly bush and half standard.

If we had known what we know now we would have bought all standard. For this reason. If you have standard fruit trees in an orchard you can graze geese, sheep, pigs, and other animals underneath. Nobody ever tells you things like that: you have to find them out for yourself.

We planted four bush apple trees, two pears, two plums, two standard cherries. Later we put in two more cherries and a crab apple, and a row of six espalier apples and pears, and the latter —although planted a year later than the first batch—are already bearing. But it will be another year or two before we really have enough apples and pears. It's a long job.

I must boast a little in the matter of these fruit trees though, in the way we gardeners do. . . .

Our soil is hardly soil at all: particularly where we established the little orchard, which was at the top of what we called The

Hill. There, under the bracken, is just a coarse sand, with hard red crag underneath: about the worst soil you could find anywhere to establish a fruit tree: particularly an apple.

But we had Michael's trailer-load of muck. We dug a big hole for each tree and carried a baby's-bath full of muck or two for each hole. (We could not afford to buy a wheelbarrow at first.) We planted the trees over the muck. The bracken between the trees we cut with a scythe, but otherwise left the ground.

Now at the same month a neighbour planted trees, from the same nursery, in exactly the same type of soil. Last year he grubbed his trees up because they had made *no growth at all*. In spite of the fact that he dressed them heavily every year with artificial manures. *Our* trees (how smug can you get?) have grown remarkably. They have grown as fast as it is possible for fruit trees to grow and not take off.

The reason? Well—at least one full wheelbarrow load of either pig muck or cow muck or horse muck dumped down around each tree every year. And also bracken. Tons of bracken. When the Forestry Commission cut acres of bracken one year in their pine plantation nearby I went and got several tons of it and piled some of it up high around the boles of the trees. It had all disappeared in a very few months—rotted away —but the soil is there. If you look at the soil around our apple trees now you won't find coarse sand and red crag rock. You will find a lovely friable loam, full of earthworms, as fertile as the best fenland. We've *made* that soil.

Soft fruit—that is something you *can* have without waiting too long. And as we hacked away at the undergrowth we began to discover soft fruit bushes that had been there all the time. In the little back garden of one side of the house were six good black currant bushes, and these we cleared and pruned and manured. In a corner of the front garden—it was not until we had hacked a way to them that we even knew they were there —were four gooseberry bushes. These, too, we cleared and pruned. We heavily pruned the old neglected apple trees in the bottom of that front garden. We had to do this practically with a book in one hand and the saw in the other—but we soon got

We Get a Cow

the hang of it. Those trees repaid us that first year (for that and for a few barrow loads of muck) by yielding heavily. But they did not produce, and do not produce now, anything like enough fruit for our requirements. It seems to me a shameful thing that anybody should live in the country and have to buy fruit.

Now what with this, and the gardening, and completely re-decorating the inside of the house (Sally comes from a family which has a tradition of completely redecorating every house any of its members move into) and earning a living, it may be imagined that we had enough to do.

The earning of the living came last. The money from the sale of *Jenny* was nothing like it might have been, and after the various fish that attend such funerals had had their bites there was very little left for us. The fruit trees—the tools—the odd junky bits of furniture—the poultry—a hundred and a thousand odds and ends—all cost money. We didn't know it then, but we were changing from an industrial to a peasant economy. We were being forced into it by the remoteness of the place in which we lived. And we had to acquire somehow the thousand and one articles necessary for the peasant life. The sort of property that every real peasant inherits from his parents.

Living aboard a boat we had had no furniture: not a stick. Living in two large cottages we found that we needed a lot. We were lucky in getting in towards the beginning of the con-sumer-state boom—when every working-class family was throwing out of doors the good old solid furniture that had done them and their ancestors so well and so long, and replac-ing it with chain-store rubbish—uncomfortable and incon-venient to use, jerry-made to last for a year or two, ugly and meretricious to look at. But "modern". "Streamlined" in case anybody might want to rocket to the moon on it. We bene-fited by this revolution of the common man, in being able to buy good old solid stuff which Sally could re-cover, or repaint, and make as good as new. (There is, while I am on the subject, a furniture shop in a nearby town which exults in the name "DAINTY HOMES". Pardon me while I throw up.)

But there we were—very broke, and getting broker by the

day. I had to make an infrangible law, which I keep to this day, of working at money-grubbing for at least half of each day. And I suppose, that including the days—and weeks—when I am away from home I probably "average" a longer working week than the ordinary eight-hour-a-day man. And by this I am not including working about our little holding. I only mean writing, recording, editing: doing the work that brings us in our income.

Meanwhile Sally was working ridiculously hard, and furthermore it was becoming only too obvious to all the world that she was going to have another baby. She is one who cannot rest while yet there is anything to be done: a ceiling unpainted, a wall unpapered, an old armchair improperly upholstered. Sally can do *anything*, and she can do it at least as well as a very good professional. But all this was keeping her away from her potter's wheel. She decided, therefore, to employ a woman to help her do the housework, and pay her out of the money which she knew she could make from potting.

We advertised in the *New Statesman*, and signed on a woman with a small daughter. The small daughter was great fun, but her mother, with the best will in the world, could not adapt herself to quite such a primitive life. She sunk into a deep melancholia, and left us two days after our second baby was born, to my great relief. I then just had to go on earning a living, and cooking, and milking (for I am anticipating my story—by then we had a cow) and feeding the pigs and the the poultry, and keeping up with the digging and planting and harvesting and food storing, and keeping the house clean or not keeping it clean, and washing up, and washing the nappies, and doing the other laundry, and looking after Jane (then three), and nursing Sally and Ann (the latter just born). In my spare time I could contemplate nature, and the Absolute, and the glories of being a married man. Mind you—Sally was up out of her lying-in bed in a very few days and bending over the wash-tub, so it wasn't all that bad.

And since then we have had a succession of women helpers: some good, some terrible. I think that I could write a treatise

We Get a Cow

from them about the neuroses of the twentieth century.

But to get back to what I might call the pioneering days: we worked *ridiculously* hard. For not only did we have to do a great number of jobs every day—but we had to learn how to do them. They were unfamiliar jobs. I had spent most of my life in Africa, where there was always a nice African man to do anything I wanted doing. Whether it was planting a fruit tree, sowing some radish seed, wringing a duck's neck, gutting and skinning a rabbit: we practically had to do it with a book in one hand and the thing in the other. This made everything ten times as difficult.

And progress seemed so slow. Doggedly, all that spring and summer, I hacked at the nettles that surrounded our house and buildings like an invading jungle, but they grew as fast as I could cut them. "Cut them three times a year for three years and they will die" someone told me. Stuff and nonsense! Cut them twenty times a year and they will not die. They will spring up with renewed vigour. Sally and I are both untidy, and in any case there was no time to be anything else. The place looked like a rural slum. I still call the Broom "Suffolk's Own Hill-Billy Country".

We kept blundering about trying to buy a cow.

It is difficult buying a cow, if you know nothing about it, and don't want to be robbed.

We went and looked at a herd of pedigree Jerseys and were offered one—a cull—at just the hundred and twenty guineas. You can buy an awful lot of milk for a hundred and twenty guineas. And you can pay an awful lot out in veterinary bills on a pedigree Jersey or a pedigree any other breed. We did have enough sense—or instinct—to steer us away from over-bred stock. Eventually we saw an "ad" in our local rag (a very good paper incidentally—far superior to most of the national press) for a Jersey house-cow. We went and saw her—she belonged to a small-holder, an oldish man, hard and tough and honest like so many small-holders, who had reared up a heifer calf from this cow and had decided to get rid of the old girl while the going was good.

41

We Get a Cow

Brownie was brown—darkish brown, too dark for a Jersey, skinny and bony and swag-bellied, a bit shy in the forequarters, not too heavily bagged, a sweet silly frightened old thing, and we bought her for thirty-five quid. She was delivered in a cattle float. And there we were.

It is something suddenly to be landed with a cow.

Brownie had just calved, but the vendor was keeping the calf. So there she was with a bagful of milk.

We had cleaned and whitewashed out the cowshed—the middle of the two compartments of the weather-boarding shed. We led her in there and I tried to milk her.

I had milked cows as a child, but not since. It came back—slowly. But milking a cow—particularly one like Brownie who is hard to milk (Jerseys are apt to be a bit slow on the titty) is hard. It is a difficult job. I have taught several people to milk since and I have found that there is only one real teacher for difficult things: *necessity*. I milked Brownie because *I had to milk her*. I believe there is no other way to learn to milk a cow. You have to sit there—until it is hard to keep the sweat of your brow from dripping into the pail—and the cow finishes the bit of grub you gave her long before to keep her quiet, and gets restive, and flicks you in the face (hard) with her hard old tail, and jigs about, and kicks the bucket, and you fumble away, and your wrists and forearms get paralytic, and only one thing keeps you at it—the knowledge that the cow has got to be milked—to the last drop in each quarter—and that she has got to be milked by you. It is no use calling on the Lord God. He won't come down and help you. You are alone—with a cow.

But when you learn to milk comfortably, which you do in about a week, it becomes a pleasant job. I look forward now to the morning and evening milking. There seems to me to be a friendliness between the cow and me, I put my head in her old flank and squirt away, and there is a nice smell, and a nice sound as the jets hiss into the frothing bucket, and I can think, and sum things up, and wonder what I am going to have for supper. In the winter it is dark and cold outside, but warm in the cow-

42

house and the hurricane lantern throws fine shadows about the building. The whole job takes perhaps ten minutes—night and morning.

The economics of it are terribly obscure, and I would defy all the accountants in the world to work them out. In the first place—an accountant would say that *labour* was the chief item. But how can you assess the cost of labour that you enjoy doing? That is where I think all accountancy falls down—flat on its face. An accountant will say that a man's labour costs—say— ten shillings an hour. Or five shillings an hour. Or what have you. But supposing a man is *enjoying* what he is doing? Then he will do it for nothing. If I were to work in an advertising agency I would want my labour to be assessed not at ten shillings or a pound an hour, but at a million pounds an hour. At least. For that is about the value that I would put on an hour of my life—knowing as I do that its hours are limited. But when I am milking Brownie I am not *wasting* ten minutes of my life. I am *enjoying* them. And therefore I do not wish to charge my time up for anything.

The other aspects of the cow economy are obscure. For example—what does the cow eat? Grass all summer, and very little else; and that we may take as being free. For the use of our three-acre grass field naturally comes in with our twenty-five pounds a year rent. Actually—it is not as simple as all that as I shall explain later on.

In the winter she must have hay, roots, and concentrates. The concentrates we have to buy and that is that. They consist mainly of oats and groundnut cake. And I have to admit, shamefacedly enough, that I have no idea what this costs me. I get a bill from Jack Hewitt the miller about once or twice a year, depending upon how energetic he is feeling in the book-keeping way, it always shakes me to the foundations, but then I know that it includes not only the little bit of food I give to the cow but also pig food and poultry food. I made a rough, jumbled, stab at working out what the concentrates for Brownie cost and came—after the most devious possible work-ings (one of the great electronic brains they have nowadays might have taken several years over it) that it averaged out through the year, winter and summer, at about a tanner a day.

Hay—I cut some rough hay with a scythe the first year in my field. That lasted me until Christmas and then I had to buy hay. The second year I cut half the field with Michael's tractor and that lasted me all that winter and half of next. This year I have had to buy all my hay—and I am feeding hay now even though it is high summer. This is because of the terrible drought *last* year (1959), the partial drought in the early part of this year (we have had floods of rain since—but too late), and the fact that I have ploughed half of my grass field up as I shall later describe. I suppose that this year, for the cow and the pony, I shall have spent, by the time the winter is over, some forty pounds on hay. But it is most unlikely that such a thing will ever happen again. Nothing but a malign miracle can make us ever have to buy hay again, and the reasons for this I shall explain in due course.

Roots—we have always managed to grow *nearly* enough, either kale or fodder beet, to feed the cow. But up to this year —not quite. This year I think we will have enough, as we have a fine piece of fodder beet on The Hill.

So all in all, our milk has certainly not been free. I would put the cost of cow food, to date, at about from twenty-five to thirty pounds a year. But this must be considered—it will get less year by year now until we may get it down to very near nothing. There is no reason at all why one should not feed a cow—ay, and two cows—*and* a horse, off five acres of land, entirely, and keep up a good milk production. But first the land must be built up to a high state of fertility—and in doing that the cow plays the most important part.

Now what do we get *from* the cow?

When she first calves, and if it is summer and the grass is green, she gives nearly four gallons of milk a day. She goes down towards the end of her lactation to perhaps one and a half gallons a day. For most of the time she is giving us from two to three gallons a day.

Now no family of our size can drink two and a half gallons of milk a day. After all—that is twenty pints. So there are various other things that we do with it.

We make all our own butter. We make most of our own cheese. By this I mean real cheese—not "cottage cheese"—which we do make as well. Further—every living thing on the place with the exception of the horse benefits from Brownie's milk. Our pigs thrive in a manner remarkable to our scientific-farmer neighbours. Our young birds thrive and grow into healthy stock by virtue of their share of whatever butter-milk, cheese-whey, milk that has been left about too long and gone bad, cream that has been forgotten and gone mouldy. Our cat and our dog benefit. And the humans benefit by having un-limited, good, untampered-with, unpasteurized, unprocessed and unbeggared-about-with *milk*. Before we had a cow our milk bill alone came to two pounds a week, and butter and cheese cost say another ten shillings. This comes to £120 a year. So—whatever the calculating book-keepers and the cos-tive cost-accountants say and they say a lot (the farming press nowadays runs an unending holy crusade to persuade people *against* being self-supporting—they want to turn every farmer into a money-grubber pure and simple), we *make* a *profit* of at least ninety pounds a year. The fact that we don't actually see the money makes no difference—we are spared having to spend it.

Then what else does Brownie give us? Well, for one thing, at least a calf a year.

Now we know that non-pedigree Jersey calves are not very valuable. But here is our balance sheet. We have *paid out* £107 10s. for cattle. We have *been paid* £149 4s. for cattle that we have sold. Thus we have made a profit of £41 14s. on the buying and selling of cattle (and rearing of calves). Added to this we still have Brownie cow, and she is at present giving us nearly four gallons a day. Her last calf, born a fortnight ago just before Sally's latest baby, proved, alas, a bad-doer and I knocked her on the head and her skin is drying for a floor mat and her meat is down in pickle in a large crock for feeding the pigs and fowls on. Waste not want not.

We Get a Cow

The size of the above sums is due to the fact that we bought another cow. One cow will not give you milk consistently all the year, year after year, and so you need two. We sold her again though, being in need at the time both of grass and cash. And once, when we didn't have any pigs, we bought a beef calf, reared him, and sold him at a negligible profit. A poor deal by any standard. Another lesson not to try to swim in the commercial sea.

But what else does Brownie give us? Pleasure, for she is one of the family. It is surprising what an affection we feel for the old creature. Fertility—for her dung is the basis of all our husbandry. She is the cornerstone of the arch of our economy. Everything we eat is enriched by either her dung or her milk. Our crops flourish because of the priming-pump effect of her manure. Our animals—and she herself—flourish because of the flourishing of the crops. She is the prime-mover of a beneficial circle of health and fertility. I know this sounds like a lot of crankish clap-trap and fiddle-faddle. It is not though. It is true and very easily verifiable.

But to get back to the tortuous line of my narrative. Having bought the cow, on the 30th of August 1957, we found that we had a lot of other things to do. In the first place—we couldn't possibly consume four gallons of milk a day and we

hadn't learnt then about turning surplus milk into cheese. We had to get some other animals to feed it to. We could scarcely feed it back to the cow—for that would somehow be unseemly. So we had to buy pigs.

In the second place—what were we going to do with all that dung? We would have to extend our gardening and farming activities. Brownie forced us, a long way, along the road that we had never planned to travel: the road to self-sufficiency and a peasant economy.

4

The Vegetable Kingdom

The British Empire is said to have been formed in spite of the British Government. Territory after territory was forced on to an unwilling Raj. As each new area was swallowed up—so it was necessary to conquer or incorporate another in order to consolidate the frontiers of the first. The Government did not *want* any more sterile slabs of Africa, or unruly princedoms in the Far East.

It was thus with our "farming" activities at the Broom.

The cow was necessary to save us the milk journey. Having got the cow—pigs were necessary to avoid wasting the surplus milk. Then more land had to be broken up to grow food for both the cow and the pigs. And as each new piece of land was brought under the spade new "frontiers" were created—new foci for invasion by the hated spear grass, bracken, nettles, and other weeds with creeping roots. The temptation always is to push these "frontiers" back—by digging up another slice of land. Then Brownie went dry and the milk-slog started again —so we bought another cow. Then Brownie calved again and we had two cows in milk—and so we kept a calf, in fact we kept two calves. We milked one cow and let the calves suck the other. Thus for a long time we had four head of cattle: it even rose to five at one time. Then we found that we had so much land broken up that we needed something to help cultivate it and we bought a horse. Then, having the horse, we found that we needed to improve our grassland and we have had to break that up too. Thus colony after colony has been added to our already overburdened administration!

The Vegetable Kingdom

But to get back to the summer of 1957.

We concentrated largely on establishing fruit trees that year: we planted sixteen altogether—four bush apple, two bush pear, two standard cherries (there was already one big old cherry tree in the back garden), three standard plums, one greengage, one walnut (which the pony has since stripped about three times), an almond which died, a mulberry and a bay. The two cherries died but the next year we planted two more—this time in the front garden and they have both taken. Also a crab-apple tree and six espalier apples. We planted most of the fruit trees at the top of The Hill because we thought, erroneously I now believe, that there would be less frost up there.

We have taken layers from the gooseberries and cuttings from the black currants, and different people have given us odd bushes like red currants and white. Every year up to this year we had a good crop of black currants from the old bushes; but this year they were a failure owing to a plague of green fly that we simply could not cope with.

The black currants have been a great standby for jam and jelly. The gooseberries have never been enough, alas. But more bushes should come into yield next year. We get a few dishes of gooseberry pie and gooseberry fool during the summer, and make a few pounds of jam; but we would like to bottle a lot of them and I should like to make five gallons of gooseberry wine for a start!

That first year we concentrated hard on the vegetable garden, and we were ignorant but keen. And surprisingly successful. Much failed: spear grass overthrew our strawberries and raspberries (we have never yet succeeded with them—we will!), peas are always attacked too hard and too early by birds (*next* year we are always going to do well with peas. Meanwhile we have to make do with a few feeds a year of our own—and a few more feeds presented to us by a nice neighbour). Brassica—the cabbage tribe—have never really flourished (again too many birds) until this year. This year I believe we have won the brassica battle. Nevertheless we have always had *nearly* enough winter greens. But never enough brussels sprouts. I do not think there is such a thing as enough brussels sprouts. Just as I do not think that there is such a thing as enough onions. All one can hope to do is to grow an enormous amount of these things and make them last as long as possible and then go without them. (Note. We harvested the onions since I wrote this, and strung them, and I think this year we *will* have enough onions.)

The bigger half of Goose Bit (if one half can be bigger than another!) we put down to kale: marrow-stem and hungry-gap. We planted this out from a seed bed and it was a laborious process. The hungry-gap` was indifferently successful: the marrow stem good. It was not good on the scale that the kale of the surrounding farmers was good. But, remember, this land of ours had as yet had no manure on it (when we planted the kale we did not even have a cow) and we have never used artificial manure.

This failure to use artificials is not "crankiness". We have never had any ideological objections to them. It is simply this: our aim in farming our little bit of land is to grow our food for nothing. If we spend money on buying artificial manures we are not doing this. Charity begins at home, and although I have no doubt that the directors and shareholders of Messrs. Fisons and Imperial Chemicals are a most deserving charity, they are one that we do not intend to support.

Also, a thing that we did not realize before we started living here but we realize now, is that food tastes a lot nicer if it has been grown with natural and not artificial manure. We do not notice this—until we go away from the Broom. Then we find the vegetables terribly tasteless. Recently it has been discovered that food grown "organically" has a different chemical analysis to food grown "with artificials". Whether better or worse is not stated but at least different. If we were growing crops to sell to the public (who nowadays do not seem to give a damn what they eat provided that when they buy it it is all wrapped up in pretty plastic wrappings) we would certainly use artificials and plenty of 'em. But, growing food for ourselves we set a higher standard.

The Vegetable Kingdom

Our vegetable year goes something like this.

Shallots should be planted on the shortest day and harvested on the longest. You plants the bulbs of course, and they grow regardless, and nothing seems to happen to them. We use them in default of onions—and for pickling. We always pickle a lot, but never enough. Pickled shallots are so nice with bread and cheese for supper that invariably they go. They never last the year out, but then few things do.

Parsnips we drill in February—but again never enough. The fact is—it is seldom that we have enough land prepared for them at that early hour, and therefore do not get enough in. Only on one year did we have enough to last us the year *and* have enough left the next February to make wine of. Surprisingly parsnip wine is one of the finest, and next year we are *determined* to grow enough of these useful roots. This year we have enough, I should think, to furnish our stews throughout the winter, but not enough for wine.

Under cloches one can start off spinach and carrots in February, and possibly transplant winter lettuce. There is a thing called lamb's lettuce which is a great stand-by for salad-stuff in the winter time—true lettuce we find is a bit of a dead loss then, cloches or no.

During January and February there should still be plenty of green stuff to eat: broccoli, cabbages, brussels sprouts (which grown on muck and picked fresh are glorious), and leeks which are a great stand-by. Leeks are another thing that it is hard to have enough of. Then, for really foul weather when you do not wish to go out and get your fingers frozen picking greens, we have salted runner beans.

In March, during our first year, we established an asparagus bed. This has proved a wonderful stand-by, for we start to pick it during April which is in the heart of the "hungry gap". It supplies us with *almost* enough fresh vegetable from April to June, and we eat asparagus then until—amazingly—we get tired of it.

Another hardy perennial is rhubarb, and that was one of the legacies left us by our predecessors. We found various plants of rhubarb hidden among the nettles and tall grasses and transplanted some in the borders of Goose Bit where they very soon became hidden by nettles and tall grasses again. We did not realize then that it is essential, for any perennial crop (or crop that stays in the ground year after year) to get the land perfectly clean of spear grass and nettle roots before planting. This year we have planted a fine row of rhubarb right across one half of Goose Bit and next year will certainly have enough for winemaking as well as to eat. It is another thing that it is hard to have enough of.

Onions we either establish by "sets" or plants. The first year we grew some of our own plants, but lately we have been buying them. This year we bought six hundred autumn-sown plants from a neighbour for ten bob and have just harvested (although it is now early August—but we lifted them early because of the incessant rain which we were afraid might rot them)—several good wheelbarrow loads, which—strung up on strings as we do them because they look so nice hanging in the kitchen—should last us *nearly* until onions come again. If they don't—well then there are leeks and shallots to make out with. We must try some "Welsh onions" some day.

In March we start potato planting. We plant a few earlies and later a lot of main crop. We generally try a row or two of earlies under cloches in February, but it does not seem to make much difference in the end. Sometimes they get nipped off by frost but they always struggle up again. We generally start lifting a few in June. Someone told me that the time to plant potatoes is when you lift them—in the autumn! They pointed out that self-sown potatoes always stand up to the frosts of the winter and produce early tubers in the spring. Being willing to try most things I intend to try this. Certainly you cannot get your teeth into new early potatoes early enough after the desert of the winter.

Main crop we put in later, when there is no danger of frost. We plant a hundredweight or two of seed, and this produces enough for the house for the year and—if it is two hundredweight and not one—enough to boil up some for the pigs.

Next year we intend to plant many more than this, to cut out buying barley meal altogether for pig-fattening.

Many people say: "why bother to grow main crop potatoes, when they are so much work to grow and so cheap to buy?" Well, in the first place they are *not* cheap to buy. They are cheap this year, and next year I imagine they may be cheaper; but last year they were a terrible price. You can spend an awful lot of money on potatoes. Besides—our potatoes taste better than bought ones. They are not flogged to tremendously high yields by quantities of artificial fertilizers. They grow naturally in good manure. We respect our stomachs—if we respect nothing else.

Secondly—they are not such a labour to grow. For we use the horse. We plough the ground, plant, and lift, by horse-power. But that comes later in my story. That first year we did it with the spade and the fork. The next year we used a "jalo" wheel hoe—with a ridging attachment.

While I am on the subject of spuds I must say that this year—when I was travelling through Sussex in the pony cart (Sally and I made a three-week trip from Kent to Somerset) I caused to be made by a blacksmith a potato planter of the kind used in the south of England. A kind of steel wedge which you tread into the ground—drop a potato into it—open the jaws of it by pushing together the two handles—thus leaving the spud under the ground. I intend to try a new way of planting.

Instead of dropping the spuds in a plough furrow and then ploughing them in as I have been doing I shall mark out stations for each plant by drawing lines crossing each other at right angles with the wheel hoe and then I shall plant the potatoes at the intersections of the lines. Thus I will be able to wheel the wheel-hoe with the ridging attachment on it both ways—up and down, and across. Thus my plants will be cultivated on all sides with the minimum of hand-hoeing, and each plant will be isolated on its own little hill. Whether this will be a good method of doing it or not I have yet to find out. Certainly it will be a new method, for I have never heard of anyone else trying the idea.

Swedes we generally grow as a field crop for the cow, and

there are always enough for the few we need for the house. Carrots were good this year—bad last. They get troubled by fly. We could guard against this with some stuff with the lovely name of "whizzed napthalim" but we don't bother.

We don't bother to do a lot of things in our garden. We let things take their chance, and every year some crops are good and others are bad; but at least there is always enough to eat and we always get a *taste* of everything. If we did all the spraying and sprinkling and dusting and fumigating that one is told to do in the books we would spend a fortune on chemicals and have no time left over for anything else. In fact—growing a big variety of crops and never the same crop two years on the same ground, and heavily manuring with the dung of a variety of animals, seems to give our crops the strength to resist most pests and diseases. Only sometimes do we come a cropper, as we did last year with onion fly, and this year with the blasted green fly on the currant bushes. All right then—not very much currant jelly—but there are other things. Some wild crab-apple trees nearby promise a good crop.

Peas we have never yet taken enough trouble over. They want very carefully guarding from birds and we have never had the time to devote to them. We always get some—and they are delicious; but never enough.

In May we sow sweet corn, and we get the new early-maturing varieties that always ripen in our sorry climate. We sow a lot of this—last year we had thirty yards by six of it and it was a bumper crop. We start eating it in the latter half of August and eat like mad until the end of September. It is quite delicious, and wonderful for feeding a multitude if one descends on you. Then—we harvest the rest and store it, by a method which I shall describe. We eat sweet corn—*nearly* as good as new—throughout the year.

Autumn-sown broad beans come in after the asparagus—for we eat them long before they are "ripe". We eat 'em pods and all—the immature pods cut up with the beans inside them and cooked and they are delicious. Thus broad beans go on providing us with food for three months or so.

The Vegetable Kingdom

In May we sow cucumbers—they have been fine up until this year, when moles undermined them and there was too much wet. We have tried pickling them but have never succeeded in finding a good recipe. They are always too vinegary. I wonder what Russian salted cucumbers are like? We must try them some day. Meanwhile our cucumbers have up to this year given us the making of salads for at least high summer and autumn. Capsicums, peppers and chillies; we have tried them all and they all grow. This last year though, because of the pony trip, we did not have time for these fal-lals. Globe artichokes we put in the first year but they died: killed by disgusting little greenfly that clustered about the stems just under the ground, brought, as I think, by ants. If ants have anything to recommend them I do not know what it is. Disgusting little fascists. We have planted some more, and they bid fair to crop next year.

Red cabbages are well worth growing. The people around here grow a few for pickling, but we eat them as a vegetable. Sally cooks them by shredding them up with a couple of big onions and a couple of cooking apples, adding salt, fat and a bit of sugar, a couple of tablespoons of vinegar, and cooking very slowly for three hours. Wonderful with rich meat such as duck or goose. You must sow seed in the autumn—although we did succeed once by sowing seed in the early spring under cloches. We often buy or get given brassica plants, but red cabbage are seldom obtainable.

The bean tribe are a tremendous stand-by. Runners we grow in large quantities and salt down two enormous earthenware crocks full. Furthermore we live on them fresh from August onwards for a long time. French and stringless are like runners only better, and I think we may go over entirely to stringless. Haricot beans of various sorts we have tried side by side in an effort to find the best variety for our purpose. We ripen these off, dry them and thresh them (we must be about the only people in England who still use a flail), store them in bins, soak them overnight and then cook them with pickled pork. They are like tinned beans only about a hundred times nicer.

Marrows we grow of course, and they store happily until

after Christmas and improve on storing. Squashes and pumpkins make a change.

We generally put in four dozen tomato plants, which we buy from a nursery for thirty-six bob. Last year we ate ripe tomatoes from August to Christmas (the green ones keep on ripening indoors) and also bottled sixty-four pounds of fruit and twelve pounds of juice. This was *nearly* enough to keep us in tomatoes through the year. And we also made forty pounds of green tomato chutney and thirty pounds of green tomato pickle. The pickle proved to be far nicer than the chutney and we shall make far more of that this year. But I must point out that last year was a drought year and the finest year for outdoor tomatoes I should think that we have ever had. This time we look like catching a cold, as they say hereabouts. But we will have some.

Celery we bang in in July or August, again buying the plants from a neighbour. It lasts from the first frost until the really filthy weather after Christmas, when it goes soggy and we get fed up with it—although it is still good for cooking for a while. Brassicas we generally buy, or get given, as seedlings. Any real gardener will sneer at this dependence—why don't we grow our own seedlings? Well, we haven't got time, that is why. And it is no harder for a neighbour to bang in another foot or two of seedbed and give us some—maybe in exchange for a dead duck. Or else the few pennies that seedlings cost at Ipswich Green Market save an awful lot of messing about, and sprinkling flea-beetle powder.

In August there are late sowings of things—carrots and kale and spinach and lettuce. In October we put in broad beans and will this year try peas. We must win the pea battle somehow.

Thus there is food to eat right through the year, in the vegetable line, in considerable variety, and of high quality.

It is a lot of work. For we don't grow just *some* of our vegetables: we grow *all* of them. What we don't grow we don't have. Therefore we need large beds and a lot of digging. But our light land is easy to dig, and—as we slowly rid it of spear grass —is easy to cultivate. We have developed labour-saving ways of doing most things. To rule straight lines for drilling for example—we use the wheel-hoe with a plough attachment. We merely walk along at walking pace and push it. And if the lines aren't dead straight—so what? The stuff will taste as good. We hoe partly with the wheel-hoe. I dig extremely quickly with a big fork. I make a *stakhanovite* operation of it. It's no use standing about. We ignore most of the rules in the books. The books say you mustn't manure this crop or that crop. We treat ours all the same. Every time we dig the ground we bang in a few barrow-loads of manure. Our roots do *not* "fork"—it's a lot of hooey. Weeds do not frighten us—except spear grass. Annual weeds we do not mind. We let them grow among a crop, then suddenly get fed up with them and walk through and hoe or pull, and the weeds die down and form a lovely mulch.

Last year—the year of the Great Drought—made us install an irrigation system, and in the dry early part of the year (this is the driest part of England) Goose Bit gets well flooded.

Moles are a terrible menace, for high fertility attracts earthworms, and the latter attract moles. If I could press a button and destroy the last mole on earth—boy would I press that button! They root along underneath rows of new seedlings and disrupt the lot. I used to trap, but found that the labour expended was out of proportion to the number of moles caught. Next year we will see what a little poison can do.*

*Thirteen years after:

I've changed my mind about moles. I don't know why but they just don't seen to worry me any more and the little occasional damage they do is probably outweighed by the good.

5

Back to the House

Yes—back to the house.

For the house is—or should be—the firm base for all the campaigns outside: somewhere to fall back on, and recuperate, and attack from again.

But, alas, the Seymours are really not nature's house-dwellers. We are really gypsies, or nomads, or rovers. Until we moved into the Broom I had never, since childhood, spent six months in one place, and Sally had led a Bohemian sort of existence during her short life. Our house is apt to look like somewhere where we are camping for the moment; and this is the antithesis of what a peasant family's house should be.

But Sally works very hard at the house, and she has a great way of whopping a paint brush or a hammer into the hand of anybody who comes and stays with us for more than a little while.

There are twelve rooms inside our house—fourteen with the lavatory and bathroom. Therefore there are seventy different walls and ceilings. Sally will not be happy until the last one of these has been laboriously scraped, and filled with plaster stuff, and prepared, and then either painted or whitewashed or papered. To me it is a terrible *bore*. But I like the results. In what I might call our *drawing-room*—the living-room of the cottage which was empty when we arrived—we had the happy idea (I claim it as a matter of fact!) of getting brass-rubbings done by a fifteen-year-old boy who lives near us from the brasses in the local church (and they are very fine ones) on

strips of ceiling paper. These Sally then papered one wall of the "drawing-room" with, very skilfully so that they are all the same height, and pious ladies and gentlemen of the past and their several issue now look gravely down at me as I write.

We could never afford to have a builder in (we did once as a matter of fact and he charged us fifty pounds for installing some taps), but we have occasionally had a little help from outside. It is not that we *cannot* do the work. We like to imagine that we can do anything that anybody else can do. It is just that we have not got time. If I could stay at home always, and work an eight-hour day at money-grubbing and no more, I think we might have managed everything. But I am apt to go away occasionally for weeks at a time, and very frequently for days, and the routine "farming" work accumulates and then I can do nothing else when I get back. For we have tried never to neglect seasonal work in order to do work that can wait. The work that can wait—just waits, and goes on waiting for years.

We employed a young student the first year to redecorate the living-room of the side of the cottages which had been occupied when we came.

This is now our living kitchen, and the room where we all spend most time. It has a fine big kitchen table in it, three armchairs which we bought from junk dealers and which either Sally or her mother (who visits us from time to time) re-upholstered and covered, and eight kitchen chairs—about the only new furniture that we have bought. The old brick floor is bare, and looks fine when it is scrubbed.

When we came there was one of those horrible shiny coloured open fireplaces in it with ovens at the side. Neither fish, fowl, nor good red herring. Lots of country people were caught out by those stoves after the war: they fell for them because they looked "smarter" than the good old black kitchen ranges. They are completely useless, and the scrap merchants of Britain have reaped a fine harvest, for every householder who can afford it has had his pulled out.

The old-fashioned coal ranges were fine, but of course you had to light them every day. Our shiny model neither cooked properly (bread baking was a battle against the oven), nor did it heat the room in winter, nor did it stay in at night, nor was it economical with fuel. Also, although nearly new, it was already falling to pieces.

We gave a lot of thought to what to put in instead. A farmer neighbour has a stove that we would have given a lot for: a big long old iron range especially made for export to Canada—wood-burning, and capable of burning quite large logs. It is when you have to saw up tiny logs that wood sawing becomes a bind.

But we could not find a decent wood-burning range. True a friend gave us a fine little enclosed heating stove called a "Forester", that burns nice long logs and keeps in all night. But you cannot cook on it.

We thought of ripping our beastly "modern stream-lined" monstrosity out and just having a large open fireplace with a big log fire in it, cooking-pots slung over it on a hake, and a spit to roast fowl and flesh on in front. I am not sure now that this would not have been our best choice. I have seen open peat fires in the west of Ireland which seem very satisfactory and labour-saving. You get constant hot water—from a huge old black pot kept permanently slung over the fire—and what is wrong with that? You can bake bread in a round iron pot. Nothing looks finer or more cheerful. By making a big fire you can create a big heat in the room. Nothing is more economical—and if you burn wood, not peat, you can burn really big logs, and we can get an awful lot of wood for nothing.

But—to come to the grand anti-climax after all these romantic yearnings for the fine and the primitive—we ended up with an Aga.

We shelled out a hundred and forty green pound notes for a beautiful shiny Aga, which sits silent and brooding as though it has some atomic pile in its belly. It almost never goes out, it keeps the water beautifully and constantly hot, it will boil a kettle in a few moments at any time at all, night or day, it is marvellous for making bread and—an enormous economy—it is fine for boiling up potatoes for the pigs. Before we used to boil potatoes and other swill in an outside copper which we bought for half a crown. This was a terrible chore in a day which already had too many chores. Now, every night, we simply put a big iron pot full of spuds and water in the slow oven, and take it out in the morning when we make the early morning tea. The great objection to fattening pigs on potatoes —labour—is out.

And at any time of the winter or summer, our living kitchen is warm to go into, there is a fine hot cupboard for drying clothes, and the stove is *fairly* economical with fuel, which of course we have to buy.

So all in all, I think that perhaps we made the right choice— in spite of the hundred and forty nicker that would have been useful for quite a lot of other things.

The larder in the east side of the house we use just as a larder. As well as the usual stores it generally has a big sack of sugar in it, and a sack of wholemeal flour, and a row of big tin canisters which contain dried beans and sweet corn and things like that, and this very day on which I write we were installing bottle racks under the shelves in which our various vintages can lie on their sides maturing. We bashed a hole in the outer wall of this larder, and took the glass out of the existing window and re-placed it with wire gauze. How food was kept fresh in it before I have no idea.

The long and narrow kitchen, or scullery, on the east side is our working kitchen.

It already had a good big sink with hot and cold water taps; we blocked the doorway that led from it into the lavatory for few things are more demoralizing than preparing food while you gaze through an open lavatory door. We filled the door space up with deep shelves, and fitted a great long draining-board in front of them. We made access to the lavatory by bashing a hole in from the bathroom. A friend was foolish enough to come and spend the week-end once and before he knew where he was he had built a magnificent and colossal dresser which takes up the whole of one wall. This is an enor-mous help. For our kitchen is not just an ordinary kitchen in which cans are opened and ordinary dishes cooked. It is a food factory. Large quantities of food of various sorts are prepared there for storing, or bottling, or wine or jam making. It always has a fine smoky smell, for up above one's head are slung big hams and sides of bacon. There is a barrel of vinegar at one end of the dresser and a pin of our wine at the other.

The drainage from the house goes to what I believe is known as a French drain—which is a covered pit down in the field. It gives absolutely no trouble at all, never has to be emptied, and except that it works just as well might not be there. Sewage is one thing we do not have to worry about—about the *only* thing I should think.

The scullery kitchen on the west side is the laundry.

There is an old-fashioned copper in it, than which nothing can be more effective. A very few minutes of fire under that is enough to bring the most gargantuan wash to the hubble. We have a "dolly-tub", which is only to be found in museums nowadays I imagine, and a "dolly-peg"—made by a turner friend of mine in Boston—to stir the wash with. He calls it a "working woman's piano". There is nothing like it for developing the bosoms. Generally whichever female "help" happens to be living with us currently, paid by the money Sally makes for her pots, spends quite a lot of her time developing herself over that dolly-tub. Laundry, to my mind, is one of the biggest problems of living in a cold climate. It is a tremendous job, and there does not seem to be an easy way out of it. Commercial laundries are fabulously expensive, and I am told "ruin the clothes". Electric washing machines are expensive too—both to buy and to run, and we haven't got any electricity, anyway. Hand-washing is laborious and seemingly never-ending. Nappies and children's clothes make up the most of it, so I suppose it is a problem that is at its worst with young families.

The west larder is the dairy. Its shelves carry big earthenware crocks in which milk is gathering cream, bowls of cream waiting to be made into butter or sometimes eaten with fruit, and cheeses being stored.

Its other shelves, in the autumn and winter, are piled high

with kilner jars and jam jars, and home-filled tins. I must say it is satisfying at the end of the summer to see shelf after shelf absolutely loaded with jars and tins full of good fruit and jam and other foodstuffs. It gives one a feeling of hope that at least one is likely to survive the winter.

At times one end of the floor of that larder, which was years ago tiled for that very purpose, is piled with bacon and ham being dry salted. And under the shelves are big stoneware Ali-baba jars containing pickled pork and other meat, salted beans, and sometimes salt herring.

Of the two small rooms tacked on to the west end of the house the front one is Sally's pottery. For years she tried to work in the big brick shed, but we could never keep it warm in the winter in spite of the most astonishing central heating system I put into it and which cost me fifty bob and an awful lot of swearing. Also—it is hard for a housewife to work away from the house. She can work in her present pottery and hear the latest baby howling if it starts to howl. My own attitude to babies always has been: "keep them out of earshot—at all costs!" But that is not a mother's way.

The rear of the two added rooms is sometimes a guest bed-room, sometimes a lying-in chamber, or labour room, as occasion seems to demand.

And then there are the four little upstairs bedrooms, in which we mostly sleep.

The fabric of the house is fine, in spite of the fact that it is at least a hundred and fifty years old, and the interior of it possibly a lot older. When I hear that such and such a fine cottage, or row of cottages, has been condemned because it is "at least seventy years old" I am amazed. I know plenty of houses that are three hundred years old—and still as habitable as they were when they were built. I do not think that a good house should *ever* be pulled down. Nobody goes and pulls the Tower of London down because it is old. Our buildings are our history. I think we could well dispense with nine-tenths of the houses put up in the last fifty years mind you, but houses built earlier than that—in the days before our taste became utterly corrupted

—should be sacrosanct, and should not be pulled down for any reason whatever.

The Broom is as good as she was when she was built. Except for her roof—and even that serves its purpose just as well.

But it is thatched with "Norfolk reed", although why it should be called "Norfolk reed" I scarcely know, seeing that it was cut within sight of the house and we are half-way down Suffolk. The front was thatched a mere twenty years ago, and is certainly good for another forty. The back though was put on sixty years ago, and is about due for a re-thatch. The ridge is of wheat straw and this only lasts for ten or twelve years and ours is well past it. But it would be useless to re-thatch the ridge and not the back—so this September we are going to thatch the back as well. We have already bought *seventy pounds worth* of reeds, again cut within sight of the house, on beds belonging to our landlord, and they lie in a huge pile outside the fence. To have cut them myself—a thousand bundles—would have taken two months, and I did not have two months.

The local thatcher would do the job for us—for perhaps a hundred and fifty pounds. But luckily we have a good friend who is a master thatcher, and who lives in Somerset and earns a living thatching mostly for the National Trust. He has promised to do it for us, in return for a holiday over this side of England with his wife and two children and that will be a very pleasant way of paying him because we would like them to come anyway.

For the rest of our "internal economy"—we had not worked that murderous semi-rotary pump for many months before we decided at all costs to get an engine. At first a blacksmith friend of mine who is rather an eccentric and a remarkable improviser sold us for fifty bob an enormous old petrol-paraffin engine that looked as if it ought to be in a museum and which sent up lovely black smoke-rings to the treetops and drove the most astonishing contraption improvised out of an old cake-crusher and an ancient brass force-pump. This was such a joy to watch, as it popped and juddered, wobbled and thumped, that we were loath to get rid of it even when we felt that its day was done. But eventually so much play developed in all the joints that the engine could be going flat-out and the pump hardly moving.

Then we bought a prosaic little one-and-a-half horse power Lister, driving a very ordinary little reciprocating pump. This fills the tank in the roof in a few minutes, and also can be turned to pumping a good stream out along the pipeline that I laid in desperation to Goose Bit last drought year. The well is shallow, but you can pump from it all day and not lower the water by an inch.

At first the well was in the open; and many is the happy day that I have spent, in a winter blizzard, with frozen oily fingers and snow drifting down the back of my neck, wrestling with engine or pump when everything was frozen solid, the engine wouldn't start, anyway, Sally was shouting for water, and the animals were bellowing with thirst.

Then a friend named Philip who came to stay paid for a moment of enthusiasm by building us a fine little oak-framed pump house, with thatched walls and a tiled roof, in which both engine and pump are housed. The oak for the frame cost us ten pounds—the rest nothing: the tiles we got off old outbuildings. If only we had known what we know now we would have used rough oak for the frame, which would have cost far less.

But even so, every autumn, I spend a day "frost-proofing" the water system. And even so, every winter, comes the day of reckoning—the day of the long icicles. . . .

Generally when I am called away to north Norfolk or somewhere, to record some reed-cutter out on a broad (it was exactly that last year in fact), and there are three feet of snow, and the ditches are frozen solid so that the animals cannot even drink from these, and we are out of paraffin because of an oversight, and out of flour because of another, and cut off from the outside world: the entire water supply freezes up solid. And there we are—without even enough water to boil a kettle.

I spend half the night, and all of the next day, working in the blizzard or the deep frost with "stilsons" and "footprints" and other esoteric devices, now hanging upside down in the well, now clinging to the roof in a gale, lighting fires here, undoing pipelines there, putting oil stoves in tanks or down wells or under little huts and wigwams that I have to build. For a couple of days—it is frozen hell. But—*this* year—it is going to be different. Or—have we heard that one before?

For here at the Broom every man has to be his own plumber. And bricklayer. And carpenter—and blacksmith— and butcher—and painter—and—yes, and dustman. For no dustman calls at the Broom, and I have to build an incinerator out of loose bricks and burn our rubbish and eventually cart the ashes off in a wheelbarrow to dump in some weapon pits that the Army dug in the pine wood and forgot to fill up.

Our predecessors solved this rubbish-disposal problem very simply. They just dumped all their rubbish in an old disused crag quarry in the Warren, or else—if they were feeling tired that day—just threw it nearby in the bracken. As I dig or plough I still turn up an unending supply of the strangest objects. While we still had the Dormobile I took off van-load after van-load of ancient rubbish to dump in a nearby rubbish pit, and also towed great rafts of wire entanglement along behind the van.

As for improvements that we have made outside the house: we have, as "funds became available", scrapped much of the awful old falling-down wire-netting fences around the house and garden and replaced them with split chestnut paling fence which we buy, very cheaply I think, from a nice basket maker and hurdle maker who lives at Wickham Market. The old wooden chicken house up on the hill, where Ken used to keep his goat, we have pulled one end out of and turned into a garage for when we have a car, and a cart shed for when we have not. The cow shed has had its doors repaired (there are always repair jobs to do with old buildings) and all the wooden buildings were tarred by a man in the village who was temporarily out of a job so we gave him that one. The big brick shed: the small room at the end of it we rat-proofed and it is our food store. The main part of it—a building some 15 yards long and 5 yards wide—we first made into a pottery but are now in the process of turning into a workshop at one end and barn at the other. It once had a brick floor, but this had fallen into complete decay by the time we got here. So I laid another brick floor in it, and can still smell the dust in my nostrils when I think of it. I removed some tiles from the roof and replaced them with glass tiles which we bought, and two of the four windows which were either open to the winds of heaven or else closed with wooden shutters before we have glazed. We built an elaborate bank of big shelves which covered one end wall, to store Sally's pots on. When she moved the pottery into the house she herself had to build another elaborate bank of shelves covering one wall of the new pottery. But the old shelves do well for storing marrows and pumpkins on, and the thousand and one other odds and ends we cannot find space for anywhere else.

Sawn timber to buy is terribly expensive; but when we had the van we used to make trips to a local small market and buy up lots of second-hand timber—much of it out of old London buildings which had been pulled down. We would store this stuff up on the rafters of the big shed—and it would all go. It would all get used up, for we could never have enough timber. At the same market we once snapped up eight long tables— which had once been school desks (I should think for giant children)—for ten bob each. For you cannot have enough working surfaces.

Our best buy to date in the snip line, I think, was five cords of oak from the Forestry Commission. This body suddenly decided to cut down many acres of twelve-year-old oak plantation, in pursuance of their policy to plant up every acre of the British Isles with either pine or fir trees. It was last year, which was a year of unprecedented timber glut in England, and they could hardly get rid of the stuff. We bought 5 cords, or about 7½ tons, for £2 a cord: £10.

It is marvellous stuff. It is piled up in a lovely tall wigwam in the yard which the kids play under, and all winter I cut the crooked poles up into logs for the "drawing-room" fire, and whenever I want a pole, or twenty poles, or a gate post, or a hundred other things, I can always cut it out of there. I should think that it will be a constant supply for us for years.

In criticizing the Forestry Commission people for their ever-lasting pine planting, one should not forget of course that they have been set up to make a profit. And if they ever *do* succeed in making a profit on this light land it will only be by planting pine trees. Hardwood trees are terribly slow-growing here. The Commission is doing superbly the job that it has been given by the Government to do: it is only a pity that the Government doesn't give it different orders. These should be: firstly—to be contented now with the land they have planted, and not to try to grab any more. Secondly to plant at least a great deal of their land with hardwood trees *even if these are uneconomic*. After all—a government is a thing that should not plan only for one generation. This would be a dismal country now if our ancestors had only planted trees which were "economic". Meanwhile the "Forestry" are very good neighbours, and they *do* do some "amenity planting": ornamental trees in conspicuous places.

Before the oak cordwood windfall I used to get permission from Michael (now and again when the pheasants were not breeding), to go into "Bob Ward's Carr" and cut ash poles, which grow there in great profusion as coppice. These are fine long slender trees and it is fun to go in there and lay about with an axe, and have them come swaying down, and then cut them into lengths and drag them out through the tangle of brambles and undergrowth, and later—when we still had the van—load them into it and bring them home across the meadows. We are searching for a light wagon now to do the same job. At first we used this ash for fence poles, and they served a temporary purpose. But all the posts we drove in in our first year are now rotted—you have only to push them with your hand to break them off. This is not the waste that it sounds, because we can still saw them up for firewood. The peasant wastes nothing! But ash, though bad for posts or any other use which involves it being in the ground, or being wet, is magnificent for firewood: "seer or green it's fit for a queen!" Oak is slow stuff on the fire when it is green but peerless when it is dry.

But we must not burn all our lovely wigwam up in a couple of years. We must still go "wooding". Alder, which also grows as coppice in Bob Ward's Carr, makes good firewood after it is dry—I try to cut some each winter to store for the *next* winter. I try to select good pieces of thinner ash branches to season for tool handles. In this sort of thing one must always be thinking for years ahead.

A great deal of our firewood we get just by lugging home dead branches off trees.

There are a lot of elm and sycamore trees about, and every big old tree gives a good harvest of dead branches every year. The big crag quarry at the back of our house contains some huge trees and is a constant mine of firewood.

The pine wood in front of the house is wonderful for kindling, for it contains larch, and larch is God's gift to fire-lighters. If you cannot light a fire with dry larch twigs then you cannot light a fire. The pine itself is not much cop for burning—nor for anything else that I can think of except pit props which is what it is grown for. As more and more pit props are steel ones presumably the demand for pine will disappear. But in years to come, when the pines come to their full size, presumably they will make deal.

It may be wondered why we want so much wood, seeing that we have got a coke-burning Aga. Well, what I have been calling the *drawing-room* (there is something terribly dated about that word—but what other can I use? It is the room to which the grown-ups *withdraw* to get away from the children, who are not allowed in it very often) is heated by a small open fireplace, and in that we burn nothing but wood. And Sally's new pottery, where I used to write, was heated by the "Forester" stove, burning wood, but the chimney smoked so much that we took it out. This autumn I am going to raise the chimney a few feet and try it again. Then there is the copper, which is a consumer of wood. But that is easy to satisfy.

The plans we have for the future for the house and buildings are many and grandiose. A large conservatory in front of the living-room. This will make the latter warmer in the winter, be a pleasant place to have breakfast, house an old existing grape vine that has been growing over our front door on that side for fifty years, and another young one that we have planted on the other side of the door and a fig tree which we have planted, and be good for raising a few pots of early tomatoes in perhaps, a few early cucumbers, and maybe a few seed boxes so that we can gain independence from the nurseries for our seedlings. Who knows—we may one day raise our own tomato plants and save that thirty-six bob!

We intend this winter a pergola leading from the back gate on the east side of the house to the back door. This is part of the attempt to make the back of the house—which everybody sees first—look less like a rural slum. Another window in the east end of the house—a glass door leading into the new conservatory—a ripping out of the bricked-in open fireplace in the "drawing-room" to make a big old fireplace again that will burn big logs and save much sawing. We are even now, with the help of a thirteen-year-old boy who comes from the village every day to ride our pony and help me about the place, putting more shelves in the larders.

For you cannot have enough *shelves*. I just do not think there is such a thing as enough shelves.

And that is about that. After all—you cannot go on for ever improving somebody else's house. But it is foolish to live out your life in an unimproved house because it does belong to somebody else. That is cutting off your nose to spite your face.

6

Pigs

W e were forced into pigs by the circumstance of having three or four gallons of milk to dispose of every day. You just cannot consume, in a small family, three or four gallons of milk.

Also, there was an existing pigsty down at the bottom of Goose Bit—an old wheeled shepherd's hut actually. Also, working hard out of doors in the winter time as we often do, we find that we can eat an awful lot of fat bacon, and bacon and ham are among those articles of food which are fantastically expensive.

I know you can get cheap fag-ends of bacon for a shilling or

one and six a pound in some shops—the bits that nobody else will buy; and certainly we cannot produce our own bacon for that price. But we found that you can soon get tired of nothing but cheap fag-ends of bacon.

And so we went to a neighbour who keeps a few pigs and bought two weaners from him for fifteen pounds. They were about ten weeks old, hogs, and we named them, for some reason, Sodom and Gomorrah.

We had to buy food for them of course. In fact that first pair of pigs were reared and fattened mostly on bought food.

But if you have to buy all the food that you give to a pig you will not make very much profit out of it. I do not say that you will make no profit: in fact most pig-keepers do have to buy all of their food, and they do make a profit. Or if they do not they go out of business. But they make a small profit—a loss in some years perhaps and a profit in others, but on the balance a profit—and they can only do this by very efficient pig-keeping. (What they like to refer to as "a high food-conversion rate", in the manner that everybody has nowadays of making every simple thing sound complicated.) They achieve this by keeping the pigs very warm; for a cold pig uses up food for warming itself, keeping them idle, so that they do not use up food to make energy (it is often the practice nowadays to keep pigs, like all fattening animals, drugged with sedatives throughout their lives), and making them grow and fatten very quickly.

We had an edge on the ordinary commercial pig-keeper though. For we had milk. We had to buy all the other food for the pigs but we could buy very cheap food. We did not have to buy a ready-prepared "balanced ration". We could buy cheap stuff like middlings and bran, stock-feed potatoes, and the admittedly more expensive barley-meal, and lace it with milk to provide protein and fats and vitamins.

Thus we did not have to be so damnably efficient. I can think of few forms of housing for pigs less efficient, in fact, than our shepherd's hut, with all the large draughty holes in the floor and big windows to let the winds of Heaven in.

If I was a book-keeping type I would certainly not be living here at the Broom like Robinson Crusoe. I am not, and, despite sporadic efforts, I have never succeeded in doing any kind of cost-accounting at all. Once we did buy three weaner pigs, gilts, with the intention of breeding from them. Their names were Big, Bigger and Biggest. A young chap named Kim who lived near here had one of them, and he *is* a book-keeping type, or at least he can do it, and as he had an interest in the pigs, owning one of them, he worked out a very comprehensive account about them. We never did breed from them, for circumstances made it necessary for us to sell them as gilts ready for the boar. We sold them for perhaps a few shillings over the market price for their weight as baconers, and according to Kim made four pounds ten profit out of each of them. This was including labour and the milk which we gave them, and every possible other cost.

We have now found much cheaper ways of keeping pigs, in which we grow the greater part of their food. But even if you cannot do this, and have to buy nearly all—or even all—of their food I think, in fact I am quite sure, that you get your bacon cheaply.

Sodom and Gomorrah, during their lives, were a mixed blessing.

In the first place we had to carry both their food and their water an awful long way—right down to the bottom of Goose Bit. We kept the food in the food store, mixed a bucket of it up twice a day using either skimmed milk or, strangely, washing-up water. An old neighbour who had been used to keeping pigs before the Government made it practically impossible during the war, put us up to the washing-up water. And of course, it is obvious that a great deal of good nourishment goes down the drain every time you wash up some greasy dishes. We stopped using detergent powder to do our washing-up, in order not to poison the pigs, and found that, in fact, it is far better not to anyway. Our dishes get just as clean without it—particularly now we have the Aga and boiling water—the effluent from our French drain, which runs into the ditch, no longer stinks, and we ourselves no longer eat off plates each one of which has a thin, invisible smear of some chemical which undoubtedly can do you no good. And, most important of all, we are no longer helping to pay for those ghastly advertisements that deface our towns, our newspapers and magazines, and our countryside, with pictures on them of goggle-eyed women going absolutely gaga with delight at the whiteness of their whites or the brightness of their ruddy coloureds.

So we keep a bucket under the sink, and everything edible or potable goes into it. In fact our garbage-disposal problem, which before was quite a big one, is solved.

Another disadvantage of Sodom and Gomorrah, though, was that they were such athletic pigs. We had a girl working for us at the time, who was fond of pigs, and used always to feed them. Quite often, as she was taking in their food, they would push past her, and get into Goose Bit, and then we would hear screams for help, and the girl crying: "Soddy! Soddy! Soddy! Gommy! Gommy! Gommy!" and I would have to rush out and there would be a terrible chase with "Soddy" and "Gommy" careering around the vegetable garden, smashing cloches right and left, and leaving havoc in their wake. I know they did it to tease.

Now we have a neighbour named Richard, and he is a most unusual man.

He lives in a cottage as remote as ours. He came down to it from a successful life in the City, where he got fed up, and to support himself he started a rush-weaving industry—using the rushes that grow within a few yards of his door—and an oyster farm. In those days he kept pigs and, indeed, tried to be as far as possible self-supporting. He had two pigs contemporary with Sodom and Gomorrah whose names were Gog and Magog. We agreed with him to kill both of ours before Christmas, and he would help us kill and butcher them, and then he would kill Gog and Magog after Christmas, and we would help him butcher them, and we would give him one of our pigs and he would give us one of his. The convenience of this was that we could get a butcher to come and do for two about as cheaply as one, and yet we staggered our fresh pork supply.

Pigs

The butcher, a friend of Richard's, charged us a bottle of whisky. This was cheap enough, considering that he had to come a good many miles and on two days.

This butchering business of course adds considerably to the cost of your bacon. We have killed six pigs here now, and have picked up quite enough about the cutting up part of it to do it ourselves. In fact we have been doing it ourselves. As for killing them—nothing is cleaner or quicker for killing an animal than a .22 rifle. I have killed everything from a mouse to a zebra with one. I have killed I should say at least a hundred antelope with one. And I have killed some scores of oxen. In Africa of course, where they don't have so many laws as they do here, and in any case where people don't take much notice of the laws that they do have.

In England I believe it is necessary to use a humane killer, and this, in my experience, can be a very inhumane instrument. With a rifle you can stand well back from the pig who is happily and unconcernedly eating from a trough, and plonk him in the head. The first thing he knows is that he is dead. With a humane killer you have actually to place the muzzle on his forehead—and you try placing the muzzle of a humane killer on a pig's forehead. Sometimes he will let you—at other times he gets nervous and you have to chase him all round the shed.

But, no matter how stupid the law is (and God knows many of our town-made laws for the countryside *are* stupid) one is supposed to stick to it, and we are lucky now in having a friend who is a licensed slaughterer, and who has a humane killer, and who is willing to come and just do the *coup de grace* business as a favour.

Certainly far more country people would keep a pig or two in the back yard, as they nearly all used to do, if it were not for all the silly laws. And if they did—we would have a happier and healthier nation. For not only would they get ample cheap and good pig meat but also they would grow more and better fresh vegetables. They would start up again the beneficial cycle of fertility in their gardens that was cut short when they stopped keeping animals.

77

In any case, for these first two pigs a butcher came, a nice man named Bob, and we got the first pig into the concrete-floored stable which we had carefully cleaned out, and Bob humanely shot him, and stuck him in the throat to let the blood out, and Richard and I got strops into his still nervously-kicking legs, and hauled him up to a beam by a block-tackle. Then, as soon as he had bled, we lowered him into a big tub that we had bought for the purpose (it fell to pieces shortly afterwards because we let rainwater freeze in it) that was full of very hot water.

Now this water has to be exactly the right temperature. If it is too hot it softens the skin and you cannot scrape the bristles off without tearing the skin. If it is too cold you cannot get the bristles out. It has to be hot enough to be extremely uncomfortable to keep your hands in. And scraping the bristles, a bit at a time, heaving the pig half out and plopping him back to get at the different parts, is extremely arduous. Even if you know how to do it, it is thumping hard work.

We tried another way of doing it the next year. I had read in Cobbett's *Cottage Economy* (the best book you can get on living like we do) that the best way to bristle a pig is not to scald him but to cover him in straw and burn him. This we did, and I still remember Richard, with his beard waving, a glass of home-made elderberry wine in his hand, the scene illumined by the leaping flames of the pyre, dancing about throwing with his disengaged hand more straw on the flames. The scene had a strangely atavistic ring. But it was only a limited success. It blackened the skin too much and did not completely remove the bristles. We probably did not know just how to do it.

Last year we tried a new method. We hung the pigs up in the usual way but poured methylated spirits on them which we lit. We reinforced this by burning wads of old cloth soaked in meth on the ends of sticks, and then we scraped the bristles as the pigs hung up. This method I can thoroughly recommend. We did the job cleanly, it was easy, and the bacon has kept well. It is the method that we shall continue to use.

But the first year the traditional scalding was resorted to, the pig was again hauled up on its tackle—hung now from a "gamble", which is that little steel girder which hooks up at each end and keeps the hind legs open, and Bob cut down the belly, removing the guts as he did so.

Richard kept some of the intestines to make sausage skins for his wife, who was German, and is an expert at making sausages. We have not got round to that yet and so most of the less appetizing machinery was just thrown to the chickens.

The "pluck": the liver and heart and "lights" or lungs, was hung in the larder, with the caul flung over it. This is a fatty membrane which is used to wrap the liver in when the latter is, deliciously, cooked.

The animal is then split down the back—right down the centre of the backbone—swilled out with cold water, and left for the night. If there is a frost that night, so much the better.

The next day the sides are carried indoors, placed on the kitchen table (and believe me to carry one of our sides is not work for a weakling), and cut into joints. Everyone who knows that you have killed a pig expects a joint (nobody has ever sent me a piece of the joint that they have bought from the butcher but that's different. They had to *pay* for that). So you either have to keep very quiet about killing your pig, or be very firm, or end up with not much for yourself.

And then the next two days are pretty well taken up with salting, canning, pickling, and all the rest of it. But more of that later on.

We "caught a slight cold" as they say about here with our exchange system with Richard.

He did not keep Gog and Magog half as long as we kept Sodom and Gomorrah, and they were not fed on milk but chiefly on carrots. For Richard does not believe in buying pig food. The result was that the pig that we gave him was enormous—much bigger than commercial "bacon weight"; but the pig we got from him was very small. We did not say anything about this though for two reasons. Firstly because we believe —or at least *I* believe—that it is quite right that a man should pay for his experience. Secondly because by his advice and help, and loan of a very useful book (the Ministry of Food booklet on pig meat curing), and his material help by smoking our ham and bacon, Richard repaid us for the difference in weight.

At all events, the two pigs did not nearly keep us in pig meat throughout the year. We had a great influx of visitors the next summer—at one time there were twenty people sleeping at the Broom—and that put paid to the bacon. On the other hand, we could never have entertained on that scale unless we had had it. Hospitality is a virtue that has practically died out in England, killed by rationing in two world wars and also by the urbanization of most of the people. Hospitality is a rural virtue. To revive it you either have to be rich—or you have to produce your own food. We will never be rich.

Ken, the former tenant of the Broom, came down one day and helped me shift the old shepherd's hut across Goose Bit and install it where it is now: behind the brick shed. There we brought it into use as a chicken house, but few of the chickens sleep in it, because it is full of fleas. And I built a little pigsty by what I thought was a novel method, up against the wall of the cow shed.

The method I used was this. I drove in stakes at what were to be the corners of my pigsty, tacked wire-netting to both sides of them so as to make a double fence of it, and stuffed straw and dry bracken between the two fences of wire netting. Then I pulled the two fences together with small pieces of wire rather in the style of an eiderdown, with those button-things at intervals over it to hold the sides together and prevent all the feathers from falling up one end.

Then I roofed it with corrugated iron. I made it very small— one has to stoop double to get into it—just big enough for two big pigs. It is very warm and, as I cut the wire netting out of an old fallen-down fence and found the corrugated iron, it cost me nothing at all.

Our second pair of pigs—which we bought in 1958—we kept in that sty but let them run out on to The Hill to dig up their own food: root artichokes, which we had established there.

Pigs

In that way they picked up more than half of their own food, with no trouble for me. We had to feed them something: artichokes are very deficient in protein, and even milk did not make up for that. We did not seek advice on "balanced rations" or anything like that, but common sense told us that the pigs would need something like fish meal, or meat meal, to make up the protein in their diet.

But still, the artichokes certainly halved our food bill that year, and gave us very much cheaper bacon. In fact for weeks together, when there were still plenty of artichokes for them to root up, we were hardly feeding those pigs at all, and yet they grew all the time. Tyler and Whittle were their names, after a double-barrelled friend of ours.

Pigs will grow on artichokes that they dig for themselves, but I doubt if they will fatten on them. They might fatten on artichokes dug up ready for them, and probably would if the artichokes were cooked. Raw, the artichokes are supposed to be in food value as to barley meal as six is to one. Cooked potatoes are as five to one.

Cooked potatoes are probably the most economical way for us finally to fatten our pigs. But only by virtue of the Aga. This year we were able to get an unlimited supply of semi-rotten potatoes—for nothing. As the Aga is alight anyway we cooked them also for nothing, and therefore they were a cheap pig food.

We learn every year, and what we shall do this year is this. We shall buy three weaners as soon as we come back from a pony and cart trip that we intend to make in September. We shall rear these up at first on a certain amount of bought food with skimmed milk and scraps—and then turn them loose on a quarter of an acre of artichokes that we have established. Before Christmas we shall kill one of them as a "porker" (i.e. not big enough for a "baconer") and him we shall eat fresh as pork and can the surplus. Eat what we can and can what we can't. We will not cure any of him as bacon, although we might put some down in pickle. But he will ensure fresh pork over Christmas, and a good supply of canned pork.

81

Pigs

The other two we will kill, one by one, some time after Christmas—the third one probably in the spring—but just before it gets too hot for the meat to keep nicely. Of the meat of these two we will eat what we are able to fresh, of course, and make ham and bacon and pickled pork of the rest—possibly canning a little, possibly none at all. For it is the canning that is the hard work: bacon curing is simple.

Is private pig-keeping worthwhile?

Certainly from a financial point of view it is. Although nowadays it is fashionable to pretend that it is not: but this is in obedience to the *zeit-geist* or *spiritus mundi* that is trying to turn us all into automatically-fed automatons.

All the older country people who live about here remember keeping their own pigs. Their saying is that there was always "a pig in the sty and one in the pot". They all say it was that worth doing and a good idea. Most of them agree that it would still be a good idea if they did it now: in fact a better idea even because of the shocking price of meat. And yet they cannot bring themselves to go back to doing it. The nonsensical regulations in the war to see that country people, who produce food, did not get more to eat than town people, who only consume it, killed back-yard pig-keeping for good. Just as the wicked and iniquitous laws forced through by the brewers to prevent people brewing their own beer have killed, for good, home-brewing.

I doubt actually whether it would pay urban sedentary workers to keep a pig. They do not eat enough bacon to make it worth while. But if you spend half a day working really hard in the winter air you can eat—and need to eat—an awful lot of fat meat of some sort or another. And if you have to buy it from a retail shop it is very expensive. Pig-keeping pays then every time.

Why do we not keep breeding sows? Well, twice now we have started to do so. We have bought female weaners, with the intention of rearing them up, borrowing a boar, and breeding from them. Kept, as we would keep them, on our system of letting them root up their own grub (breeding stock, unlike fatteners, will live exclusively on rough food with just a dash of protein) they would be highly profitable. We could fatten two or three of their litters for ourselves and sell the rest.

But each time, when our gilts had grown up and were ready for marriage, we found that we had to go away somewhere, or *wanted* to go away somewhere, for several weeks. We can generally get somebody to come and milk the cow and feed the fowls on these occasions. But there is rather more work to be done with pigs. For example—they have to be watched so as to get the boar just at the right time. They have to be cared for properly when they farrow. So we have just sold them and, undoubtedly, we have made a good profit out of them. And we have gone on in this dependent way: buying weaners, generally for five pounds each, from a neighbour. One year we bought three weaners, fattened the lot, and sold one of them. We got just over twenty pounds for him so he paid for the other two.

Pigs pay, either to kill yourself or to sell, provided that you can grow at least some of their food, and provided that none of them get ill. For pigs can be hit very hard indeed with all sorts of illnesses. My own belief though—a belief borne out very strongly by the experience of various pig-keeping neighbours —is that *they will not* get ill, practically ever, if they are looked after in a certain way. The way is this. Pigs must not be put on the same ground that pigs have been on before—until that ground has had a rest and several crops on it. They must be kept in the open—kept as rough as you like—made to root up most of their own food—but not put on land that has recently had pigs. They must be kept moving, in fact, so that they leave behind them their parasites. As for housing—the most successful pig-keeper I know houses his in shelters made by leaning two sheets of corrugated iron up together. In the summer the ends of these little huts are left open—in the winter sacks are hung over them. He feeds his pigs hardly anything at all beyond the grass they pick up in the summer and the artichokes in the winter and a little protein. But he keeps them on the move all the time. The various worms and parasites that inhabit pigs never have a chance to complete their life cycles. For the eggs fall on the ground—and then the pigs are moved away; and the eggs will be dead long before any more pigs are moved back on to them to take them up again.

All this is an argument for *mixed* farming, a big variety of crops and stock. The parasites of one animal do not attack another, therefore you can follow pigs with, say, cows, cows with sheep, sheep with geese, geese with pigs again. Each species gets something out of the land that the others don't use, each contributes in its droppings something that the others do not contribute. You will have healthy and productive stock— healthy and productive land, and healthy and productive people who live off the stock and the land.

But this again is against the *spiritus mundi*. The Government, the agricultural supply industries, the agricultural press, all carry on a holy crusade nowadays to persuade farmers to *specialize*. One man one crop—or one man one kind of stock. And disease is to be fought off in the resulting vitiated plants and animals by more and more chemicals, and the exhausted and ravaged soil is to be mended and patched with more chemicals. This is the industrialist's method of farming—or the scientist's—the scientist who knows his own narrow branch of science and nothing else. It works. What the long range effect of it will be, on land and stock and people, is not known. What must be known is the cataclysmic disaster that would follow any hitch in the supply of chemicals.

7

The Land

———

Our field, which has the bizarre name of Star-goose, was really a mass of rubbish when we came to it.

It had a lot of coarse tussocky grass in it, patches of nettles, patches of thistles, patches of brambles and dog rose, and the first summer it grew a swingeing crop of what the people call hemlock around here—a yellow-flowered version of sheep's parsley, inedible to stock, and probably poisonous. This stuff grew as high as a man and practically all over.

If you looked a bit closer in the mat of vegetation you could see, up near the top of the field, a lot of mare's tail or what they call "cat's tail" here, and down in the middle and near the bottom a vigorous kind of vetch with pretty blue flowers. The bottom part of the field, near the ditch, grew a fine crop of reeds and sedges. The top edge of the field marched with the lower edge of the pine wood and our garden, the bottom had a ditch along it which separated it from some miles of marshes. The south end of the field, which was long and narrow, was separated from eight acres of wilderness called The Skirts—a wilderness of boggy ground, elder and alder scrub, brambles, and coarse grass. This wilderness was very useful to us because our cows could wander into it and find odd bits of grazing and thus spare the grazing in our field. It has since been, alas, cleared and ploughed up. Our field was three and a half acres.

It was obvious from the start that if we were to keep two cows, which we would need to keep ourselves in milk through-out the year, and a horse, which we had a vague idea that one

day we would like, off that one field we would have to improve it. And so I made an arrangement with my landlord that he should plough one half of it up, take a crop of barley off it, and undersow the barley with a grass and clover mixture. Thus, when the barley was harvested, the field would be covered with grass and clover.

I hacked down large patches of brambles and burnt them, cut fifty ash posts out of Bob Ward's Carr Marsh and put up a fence right across the middle of the field, and Leslie, my landlord's tractor driver, came and ploughed the farther half up, and pulled it about a good many times with the disks.

But he got only a roughish seed bed. There was far too much old rubbish—great mats of reed roots, tangled masses of vetch, water-grass roots that we knew would grow again and spear grass—for there to be much prospect of a good harvest. The ploughing was done in February, which was far too late anyway. It should have been done in the previous summer, the land pulled about most of the summer to kill the spear grass and reeds and mare's tail, left to weather all the winter, pulled about again in the spring, and then drilled with barley. Or better still a root crop.

I know *now* what I should have done with that field. I should not have had a tractor at all. I should have done my ploughing, a small strip every year, with pigs. But that is another story.

The barley was not a success. Our geese didn't help. They got through the fence, which was there to stop cows, not geese, and cut a swathe into the growing barley like an invading army. The early spring drought did not help. The foulness of the land and rough seed bed didn't either. But the pheasants did most damage. They came in like Goths. You see our field was an island of cultivation in a sea of uncultivated land. We live in what is for England the middle of a large uninhabited area, and there are no poachers. The place swarms with pheasants, for this light well-drained land is ideal for them. This estate was once one of the big classic pheasant-shooting estates in England, and five thousand birds at a *battue* was considered normal. We keep them out of our garden and vegetable patch by constant vigilance. But we could not keep them out of the barley.

There was no crop of barley. There wasn't so much as a bushel to be harvested. And, left, there was a very indifferent ley of grass and clover. But it was a great improvement on what had gone before.

That summer I cut as much as I could of grass in the other, unploughed, half of the field for hay. I cut it down near the ditch (we had a dry year and there the grass was lushest), with a scythe, and very hard work it was too. I larded that grass with my sweat. Mowing grass with a scythe depends on keeping the edge of the scythe like a razor. I am not very good at it. To cut corn you want a rough, serrated, edge, but for grass it must be smooth and wickedly keen. I cut enough grass that first summer to make us perhaps half a ton of hay, and it was good hay, and it lasted Brownie cow until Christmas, which was something. We carried it in the back of the Dormobile.

To continue the hay saga—the next year, 1958—we had had the other half of the field ploughed up—but we cut the grass of the farther bit—the half which we had put down to grass and clover. It was not a big crop and yet the hay that acre and a half made (that "half" of the field was the smaller and only about an acre and a half. Sally and I are crank peasants—not mathematicians. There are plenty of those in the world)—it made enough hay to form a sizeable little stack, to last us all of that winter and half of next.

We had this hay cut with a tractor, because Alf, the other tractor driver, happened to be passing by one day and he asked if we would like him to do it and it took him a few minutes. We enjoyed going out, Sally and I and a girl who was staying with us, and turning the swathes and making the hay and then putting it up into cocks, and later stuffing the cocks into the back of the Dormobile (a pretty unsuitable vehicle for the job, as it had a roof, but all we had got) and carrying it back to the stackyard. And there we had a neighbour named Leslie (another Leslie), who came to help us at so much an hour in his spare time because as I was going away shortly on one of my money-making jaunts, and had been going away a lot before that summer, things were getting behind-hand, and I pitched the hay up to him and he stacked it. And then together we tried to thatch it, with reeds which I got from down on the marshes. We made an indifferent job at this, and still I cannot claim that I know much about thatching. I shall know more by the time I have finished writing this book, however, because by then I shall have acted as mate to the young thatcher who is coming to thatch our house.

Of course you come up against one little problem when you have made a haystack. How do you get the hay out again when you want it? You cannot just start ripping off all the thatch and pulling away with a pitchfork, for you would soon find that—to get one forkful of hay—you would have to take the whole of the top off, and the rain would get in and ruin your stack.

So I had to buy an old stack-knife, for ten bob, because few people want stack-knives any more. Hay is baled nowadays.

Cutting a stack with a stack-knife is work that makes the sweat drip off the end of your nose in the middle of the winter.

The next year, 1959, we came completely unstuck for hay.

In the first place it was the worst drought ever recorded in England, and the grass scarcely grew on our light land. In the second place we by then had two cows, and two calves, and a pony, and they needed what grass there was.

True, Michael, our landlord, out of the kindness of his heart, allowed us to use Bob Ward's Carr Marsh for a large part of the summer, for no rent, without us asking him, just because he realized that we, like he, were short of grass. But even so—our herd of animals polished off our little bit of grass and clover as a razor shaves off a black man's beard.

Secondly—we had by then ploughed up the other—larger—half of our field, and had it down to crops.

So we made no hay at all that year. The hay we had made the year before lasted us until Christmas and then we had to buy hay (ordering it by the ton from a merchant because all our neighbours were short of hay for themselves) and shelling out fifteen green pound notes a ton for it. It broke our hearts. But not to despair. We were *still* getting very cheap milk—and we sold the calves that we had reared at quite enough to pay for a few tons of hay—and a few things else.

This year, 1960, we came unstuck again for hay. Again we were heavily overstocked. Although we had sold one cow we still had Brownie and a heifer, Daisy Bell, that we had intended to rear as a replacement. So short of grass were we though, with our miserable acre and a half of it, that we were forced to sell Daisy Bell about a month ago. It would have been far better if we had sold her before, in the spring, when she would have fetched as much (she did fetch thirty-nine pounds) and would have spared our grass. But we still have Brownie and the pony, and we are feeding hay even now—in August! One surely should not have to feed hay in the summer-time.

But a nice neighbour, a tractor driver for a big farmer but a smallholder in his spare time, had cut and baled about a ton and a half of fine meadow hay from the field where he keeps his pigs and chickens, and sold it to us for five bob a bale. As the bales are enormously heavy (the weight of bales varies a lot) this is cheap, and it is very good hay. Also, our landlord presented us the other year with a horse-drawn hay-rake, and this year he gave us permission to rake up behind the pick-up baler on one of his marshes and thus we got another half ton of hay. So we should have enough to last the winter, and did not pay very much for it.

The future should present a better picture. For it is vain to say that you are self-supporting when you have to buy hay every year. But this year we have put most of the bigger half of Star-goose down to a lucerne-clover-grass mixture, and it seems to be taking very well. We will certainly have enough hay of our own next year, and enough grazing too. But the interim hayless period was necessary while we improved the land.

To get one's neighbour to mow one's field with a tractor is certainly not being self-supporting. But I do not see any reason why I should not, in future, do the job in the good old-fashioned way, with the scythe.

All we need is the hay off an acre of land. That is quite

enough for us. A good mower should mow an acre in a day. There is no reason why I should not give up two half-days to the job a year. It is not *wasting* the time, any more than President Eisenhower is wasting his time when he is on the golf links. It is good for me to swing a scythe. If a man does not undertake some really hard and even violent manual work fairly often he becomes soft, his arteries harden, his heart weakens, he puts on fat, he develops blood-pressure, his liver gets hob-nailed—I hate to think what he looks like inside. And outside he doesn't look much better. President Eisenhower does not have a machine to play golf for him. For the same sort of reasons I should not have a machine to cut my hay for me. (All the same, I have to admit, if I could find a good little grass mower that can be drawn by a pony I wouldn't half be glad to lay my mitts on it!)

As for our other cultivations in Star-goose: last year, the drought year of 1959, we made the decision, in February again and far too late, to have most of the bigger half of the field ploughed up to grow crops on, in order to clean it a bit before putting it down to lucerne, clover, and grass.

This was not altogether a success.

Our plan miscarried for three reasons. One was the drought. Much of the seed which we planted—the kale for example—did not germinate for many weeks after we had put it in—how could it when it was just lying there in the dry dust? But the old tough perennial plants that the plough had never killed but just turned over—they began to grow again. For they had the vigour to get their roots quickly down to what moisture there was. And so I had to look on helplessly while the weeds grew —and I could not hoe them because I could not see where the rows were in which I had drilled my seeds!

The second reason was that I was away too much. You cannot farm if you are cruising around the western Midlands, as I was, making a programme for the wireless about the River Severn.

The third reason was that the ground was insufficiently prepared.

The Land

Nevertheless, in spite of all these reasons, we grew a block of artichokes at the top of the field that at least fed our pigs that year for a month or two. We grew perhaps half a ton of potatoes—scabby though they may have been because of the drought. We grew a dozen rows, seventy yards long each, of cattle beet and fodder beet, which fed old Brownie throughout the winter. We grew a couple of rows of carrots, some swedes, and some poppies, the seed of which had been given us by a German girl. We harvested the poppy seeds and still have some, and the kids love to eat them like sherbet, and we really haven't the faintest idea what to do with them. I am sure that they would be very good for something—but what?

But *this* year we laid out about ten quid on the bigger half of the field—having it ploughed, and ploughed again, and culti-vated and cultivated, and disked and disked. Every time the hated spear grass poked its leaves above the ground again the tractor came and hit it—wham! Then I harrowed it well with the pony. Then I broadcast over it, in the good old-fashioned way, twenty pounds of lucerne seed, and a mixture of white clover, cock's-foot, and perennial rye grass. And in this summer when it never seems to stop raining it is doing wonder-fully. The only weed that we have not substantially eradicated is that fossil plant—that coelacanth of the vegetable kingdom—mare's tail. This has come up again in a swathe across the middle of the field, where conditions evidently just favour it. I am pulling it out by hand, but the springy yielding roots are still there. It will come again. It has been growing there since carboniferous times.

About a quarter of an acre at this end of the field Sally and I, last February, laboriously planted with artichokes.

This end of the field had not been ploughed before, and it was ploughed once just before we planted it. There it lay in great ridges, with the dense mat of vegetation that it had had on it still poking up from the furrows. It was a terrible mess. It had not even been disked.

Every morning for a week Sally and I would get up at five o'clock, and sneak out with our spade and sack of artichoke

The Land

tubers, and I would go ahead and dig holes in this mess of a field, and Sally would come behind dropping tubers into them and covering them with her foot. Surely no crop has ever had less preparation?

Result—a dense, hardly penetrable in fact, mass of coarse green plants with huge leaves on them—*Douanier* Rousseau plants—much higher than my head. Not one tuber failed to grow, and the weeds below them didn't get a chance.

Into this the pigs will go, as soon as they are strong enough to use their snouts, and they will find their food there for most of their lives without another bit of effort from me, and they will trample all that vast amount of vegetation into the soil, and they will manure it liberally (again no effort from me) and they will leave it much as the fields of Flanders were left after a creeping barrage.

Then, the faithful Pinto will drag the heavy harrows over it (or a spring-tine harrow if I can get a section of that for practically nothing), and keep on doing it until it is levelled out again and I am ready to plant crops on it.

For that end of the field is destined now to become our permanent growing place.

I shall put a permanent fence around it, and every year it will be planted in strips like a medieval strip-system. There will be a strip of carrots, one of onions, a couple of rows of parsnips, a few rows of brassicas, a few rows of spuds, a biggish block of kale, whatever we want.

It will be cultivated by the pony. It will have to be manured by pony cart. I shall be most surprised if it does not supply us with all the vegetables, roots, and greenstuff that we and our animals require.

The Hill has also made its contribution.

For the second year that we were at the Broom we got our old ally the tractor in again and had him plough up such of The Hill as we had not planted up with fruit trees. And that meant most of it, for the fruit trees occupy just the top corner.

When it was ploughed, then, and disked a couple of times, we set about planting it.

93

The Land

The bottom edge of it we made into a vineyard.

In it we planted ninety grape vines of varieties which have been tested to ripen their fruit in the English climate. In medieval times East Anglia was a great place for grapes. The climate worsened after the Reformation, but is now supposed to be getting better (although heaven knows—this summer one would hardly think so!). At all events, other people have succeeded in growing outdoor grapes since the war and I do not see why we should not. Particularly as this light soil is perfect for them.

In any case we planted these ninety grape vines (which we bought from The Viticultural Research Station, "Summerfield", Rockfield Road, OXTED, Surrey), and most of them "took", and we let them straggle for a couple of years, and we let them straggle again this year although we should have pruned them and trained them along wires, and they are straggling even now—but they are bearing a large crop of baby grapes. Whether these will ripen or not this year is doubtful. But certainly they should next, for straggle then they shall not. They will be trained properly along wires. Then—look out for the heady product of Chateau Broom!

Above this, on The Hill, comes a triangle of stuff called Russian Comfrey.

This is the real Muck and Magic Crank's Delight!

It sends its roots forty feet down, until they get to water. It gives you three or four heavy cuttings a year—in the tropics it has been known to give a hundred tons an acre! You can feed it fresh to stock (*any* stock will learn to eat it, and once they have learnt will eat it in preference to anything else). You can make a sort of hay of it.

We feed it mostly to ducks and geese, when we want to shut these birds up for any reason and there is not much else to give them. They love it and thrive on it.

Above this area, there was nearly a quarter of an acre more land. And this, in 1958, I planted with artichokes. I bought five pounds' worth of seed tubers of a plant called *topine* which is a kind of artichoke which is supposed to be heavier yielding than the usual kind. I planted it by pushing a Jalo ridging plough attachment (we did not have the pony in those days), up and down, four times in each furrow, and it was not just hard work—it was a gigantic labour..

For before that ground had been ploughed it had been high bracken, and the tough rhizomes of the bracken still matted the soil.

Then I dropped in my tubers—far too close for their comfort (a neighbour came and told me afterwards that it was "a vegetable slum") but also too close for the comfort of the surviving bracken.

Then I split the ridges, again with the push-plough. And up came the artichokes.

Up came the bracken too; but I walked up and down as it came and pulled it out. The artichokes beat the bracken—and grew higher than my head—and then in went the pigs. They rooted it up and tramped it down. I thought they had rooted out the last splinter of artichoke tuber and the last rhizome of bracken.

Not a bit of it. Next spring—when I was wondering what to do with the land—up came the artichokes again as thick as before —and up came the bracken.

Again I had to walk through, pulling out bracken.

Again I waited until the autumn and then put in the pigs. This was breaking my rule about not running pigs two years in succession on the same bit of land, but rules are made to be broken. The pigs thrived.

And this spring, after the pigs, I made the pony drag the heavy harrow up and down that steep and rough hillside, then the light harrows, and then I drilled it with my little Jalo drill that cost me five pounds with fodder-beet seed.

Fodder beet was a mistake. Up it came, all right, but for busy people like us, in rather foul and rough ground, it was a mistake. We had to single it practically by hand, for fodder beet— like sugar beet and like mangles—comes up much too thick and you have to single it. And we had to second-hoe it. And hand weed it. And it all took a terrible *time* and other things have been neglected.

The Land

But the result? The Hill is now quite free of weeds—at least that bit of it is, and we have a really fine crop of fodder beet. I have never seen fodder beet grow better. Although we put our seed in much too late, and used not a grain of expensive artificial manure, our beet looks better than the beet of any of our professionally farming neighbours. And there is certainly enough to keep two cows throughout the winter.

I harvest it like this. Every morning before breakfast, during the autumn, I pull a wheelbarrow load, and wheel it back to the cow shed. The tops I cut off and feed there and then to the cow, who loves them and needs, at that time of the year, just that little bit of lush green food. The roots I throw over the partition into the food-store part of the cow shed, where they will lie until I bring in the last wheelbarrow load, round about Christmas, and then have to start feeding the roots.

Fodder beet is magnificent milk-producing food. With it, and good hay, and perhaps the tiniest bit of "concentrates" (corn and cake), a cow will flourish and give milk the winter through. Particularly if, like our cow, she can roam about where she will, through a big pine wood, over a three-acre field. For a cow likes to nibble all sorts of weeds and rough things and the leaves of trees, and get into herself things that probably the chemists have never heard of. Nobody knows so well what food is good for a cow as a cow.

In the summer you should get your milk for nothing. In the winter you should get it for a very few pounds. And when we have our own hay and roots and kale no doubt we will. Two or three bags of oats and a bag or two of cake will be all that we will have to buy.

Our farming of our five acres is very much affected by the fact that we are apt to go away for periods of time. This year we had three weeks' pony and cart trekking, and we intend to have some more. Last year Sally and I went off to Scotland for three weeks. Next year we hope to spend a month or two in Spain. This travelling we do because we like it, but also because we make it part of our livelihood.

If we could be purely static, or had to be—if for example I

had an ordinary job on "The Island" like most of the men around here, or in a bank or an insurance office—we would farm our five acres in a rather different way.

This is the way, in the light of the experience that we have had, we would do it. And the way that we probably *will* do it one day when we are more settled down.

We would cut up Star-goose into a number of strips, with permanent wire fences.

Into one strip, in the summer, we would turn unringed pigs. They would eat the grass and clover and turn the ground into the aftermath of the battle of Passchendaele. In the winter the pig herd would be moved on to one of the other strips—which already had been planted with artichokes. They would winter there. Another strip would be cultivated by the pony and be growing row crops. Another strip—or probably two strips—would be growing grass and clover for hay. Only a temporary ley mind you—no grass would stay down longer than three years—for the pigs would come along after three years and dig it up again. Another strip would be grazed by the cow. Another by the horse. Another by geese.

Thus the different animals would follow each other, each manuring the land in a different way, each treading it or rooting it in a different way, each adding to—not detracting from—its fertility. No one kind of animal would stay on one piece of land long enough to infest it with parasites. Our arable land would be ploughed for us by the pigs. Our grass land would be the most productive that it is possible for grass land to be: short-term grass and clover leys on well-cleaned and heavily dunged land. That little field would carry a colossal head of stock.

And the small bits of land around the house—Goose Bit and The Hill—would be put down to permanent crops like fruit, more vines, more Russian comfrey, and lucerne. Our vegetable gardening, which we now do with the fork and the spade and hard labour, would be done out on the field with the horse. French peasants do not "garden", although they eat the best and most varied vegetables in the world. They grow their vegetables on a field scale—a row of this down the field and half a row of that. Why not? A quarter the labour.

Up to now we have had a lot of pioneering work to do at the Broom. And there is quite a lot more. But when this pioneering work is all done, and only the routine, recurring, work of stockmanship, cultivating, harvesting and that is left to do, I believe that we could manage our little holding on somewhat the above lines with not very many hours of work a week.

And after all, if a family can grow all its own food, "for free", off a piece of land which is no more than that family's fair share of the land surface of its country, and have some produce left over for other people, and still have time to do other work, it is in a very sound position and nobody can say that it is not pulling its weight.

The one lacuna in our cropping is corn. Not sweet corn— that we do grow; but wheat, barley, oats and rye.

We have yet to experiment with it. If we could grow, say, a little wheat, successfully, we would no longer have to buy grain for our chickens. The latter could not only thresh but grind the wheat themselves. If we could grow barley, and thresh it which we no doubt could with a flail, and grind it (which we certainly could because we bought one for thirty bob, a little Canadian grinding mill that can be driven off the pumping engine) we could fatten our pigs and fowls for nothing. Now we buy a little barley meal just to finish them off with. It would be nice to grow oats for the cow and the horse.

If we could grow all our own wheat, and thresh it, and win- now it, and grind it, we could make bread from it. We would thus save ten pounds a year, which is what we now spend on the flour with which we make our bread.

Would it be worth it?

We will certainly not know until we try. But this I am sure of: we *could* do it if we wanted to.

8

To Preserve what we Produce

It is all very well to talk about "the fruits of the earth in their season", and very nice too; but it is nice to be able to eat tomatoes in April, or pork in August. Of course if you buy these things from a shop you can eat anything at any time of the year, but then you find you have to catch the eight-thirty every morning and go and sit all day in a stuffy office to be able to afford to do so.

If you do not want to catch the eight-thirty what you do is you grow these things for yourself, and preserve them.

Our food-preserving year may be said to begin in the winter, when we kill our first pig.

So far we have raised our pigs to bacon weight—in fact often well over it. I have no idea what our pigs weigh, because we have no means of weighing them; and to tell the truth we are not very interested in weights and measures at the Broom. We like to see some socking great hams hanging over our heads in the kitchen, and that is that. It gives us a sense of stability.

But a pig of bacon weight provides you with a tremendous amount of meat. There it is—dumped on the scrubbed kitchen table. One side of a pig, and as much as a strong man can carry. It is useless to try to describe the method of jointing it, for this can only be learned by watching somebody do it. When you come to do it yourself—as we did the second year when we had already watched two pigs being done—you stand there with the knife in your hand, a saw, and a hatchet (somebody gave me a beautiful butcher's chopper for a Christmas present) and

99

your heart in your mouth. For it is a nerve-racking operation. You must sever the carcass with quick, clean cuts, which cut straight down to the joint that you wish to sever. You can't prod and slash about, and worry the thing to pieces, for if you do you will have jagged hams and sides and other joints and they will go bad. Sally is marvellous at remembering where to cut. She remembers to count the ribs—five from the shoulder is one. But the thing is—provided you cut cleanly and boldly you will get the side to pieces somehow, and with perhaps a little cleaning up afterwards you will have more or less what you want. And, when after some practice you do it just right, you have that fine sensation of having tackled a difficult professional job and mastered it.

The head and feet and all sorts of odd bits here and there we put straight into a huge pot and boil up for brawn, or pork cheese. When it has simmered away in the slow oven of the Aga all night we haul it all out, bit by bit, with our bare hands, and pull the meat off the bones, and pull the whiskers off the bits of skin, and throw the teeth out, and the whole business is grisly beyond belief and very reminiscent of a cannibal feast. The resultant mess is put in a pot again, with herbs and spices, and boiled up, and then either put into pudding basins to cool, or else canned. Most of it of course is canned, and a big pig gives us eight two-pound tins of brawn. And believe me, it is quite something for a poor family to start the year with eight two-pound tins of brawn on the shelves. The stuff is perfectly delicious, even when it has been tinned. You can open a tin whenever unexpected guests come in the summer-time, and it is delicious, cold, with salad. And that is only one pig—we kill two. (This year we intend to kill three.)

With making brawn as with doing all the other things—this I must stress. It may be messy, it may be a lot of work. But it is far simpler to do than you imagine. In fact with brawn all you have to do is what I have described—nothing else. The books you read on the subject make it all sound so terribly complicated.

We decide what joints we want to eat ourselves as fresh roast pork, or give away; and these we cut out and put to one side. You can roughly say with a pig—the nearer the rear, the better the meat. Perhaps the most delicious part is the tender loin, which consists of two muscles that run along the underside of the backbone at the loin. Sally and I hang on to this for dear life—nobody in England would wheedle it out of us. She cooks it rolled round a delicious stuffing of sage and onions and other things and it is out of this world. And this we have found, while on this subject of preserving pig meat. In the English winter, provided you hang your pig meat in a draught—preferable outside at night in fact so that it gets the frost—it will stay good for weeks if not months. Just as it is. This year we intend to kill three pigs, as I said, and the first of these we shall eat largely like this—just as plain fresh pork. It will keep us in fresh meat for a lot of the winter.

But any pork that we do not intend to eat fresh, and that does not come under the heading of ham and bacon, we put into cans.

For this one needs a little machine called a "Homcan" machine, and I believe that if one bought one new it would cost about twenty pounds. Many Women's Institutes have them for members to borrow. We were lucky in being able to buy one for a fiver from some people in Shropshire. It is as good as new.

A booklet came with it telling us how to use it. Like all such books it makes it all sound terribly complicated. In fact all we do is this. We cut the meat into lumps—fry the lumps up with onions—then cram lumps and onions into the cans. We top the cans up with liquor over from the brawn and place them in a big pan of boiling water so that the water comes within an inch of their rims. Thus we boil them for twenty minutes. We take them out with tongs (because they are hot!) place them on the canning machine, turn a handle, and lo—they are canned. We put them into a net and, when the net is full, we dump it into the copper. There we let them boil for three hours. We then fish the net out and dump it straight in the rain butt. When the cans are cool we fish the net out, dry the cans, and label them.

And it has taken us three years to learn this lesson—to label them well, with the labels going right round the can or they will come off and we won't know what we are opening, than which nothing is more infuriating.

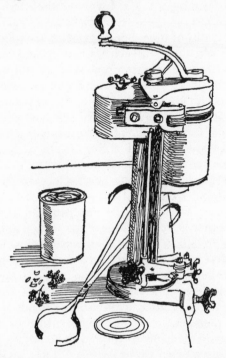

From a pig we get about, as I said, eight two-pound tins of brawn, then fifteen two-pound tins of pork, six of lard, and two of liver *pâté*. I am touching wood even as I write this—with six pigs we have not yet had one tin fail. And now as I write this, towards the end of August, there are still fourteen fat tins of what we call "roast pork" sitting in the larder, waiting to be warmed up and dished out when we are feeling particularly hungry and are too lazy to wring the neck of a chicken.

You can dispose of a pig quite easily *without* a canning machine. You would just dry-cure more, put more in pickle perhaps, and then probably learn to make sausages. Our neighbours Richard and Matilda (Matilda was a German girl), who have taught us more about preserving food than anything else, make magnificent German-style smoked sausages, that keep for ever and taste superb. Me, I would rather have them than all the canned meat in the world. The canning machine is a bit of a short way out of it, and perhaps not a very good one.

Now—the very fatty bits such as the belly, and various other strips that seem to come from nowhere, we roll up tight, tie with string, and drop straight into a crock containing salt and water. Water with enough salt in it to float a potato. Nothing else. It is as simple as that. It keeps for ever, and when we want a piece we just fish one out, soak it overnight in a change or two of fresh water, and boil it. Surprisingly it is delicious: I think perhaps the nicest part of our pig. With dried haricot beans, also soaked, it is beyond belief. On a cold winter's day it is the making of you.

The main part of the pig is left—the hams and sides and maybe forehocks or collars or whatever you choose to call them— and this you dry-salt. You can, if you wish, follow the "graduated cure": that is salt each piece for a shorter or longer length of time depending upon how long you intend to keep it. Thus the bits that get eaten first are most lightly salted, and therefore taste better. We have not got that sort of mind: we bung the whole lot in together, and try to fish the smaller or thinner bits out first, leaving the hams in until last, and hoping that it will all keep as long as we want to keep it. Which, again touching wood, it so far always has.

We sprinkle a little tiny pinch of saltpetre straight on to the meat (you are supposed to mix this with the salt but we don't) we then rub the meat hard with salt, we then pack these large and heavy lumps down in the corner of the larder well buried in dry salt. For the first day or two I go and pull them out again and rub them with salt and change them round and turn them over. If I remember to. We leave them in for from ten days to three weeks, depending on their thickness. We then haul 'em out and hang 'em up—washing the salt off first.

We then smoke them.

Richard smoked our first pig for us. He had built a brick smoking kiln, which had a patent burner that he had made, burning outside it, with a pipe to take the smoke into the kiln.

We have copied this—making use of one of the outdoor lavatories that were at the Broom. (The other one we pulled down for bricks and tiles.) Outside the lavatory we have a "Forester" stove, and the chimney pipe from the stove goes through a hole in the wall of the lavatory. We hang the meat on an iron standard that goes across the middle of the lavatory (you want something strong) and light a fire of oak logs in the stove. Result—a cloud of choking oak smoke—*cool*, which is important—for as long as we like to have it. Generally about a week—although I am beginning to wonder if that is not too long.

You needn't smoke bacon. I think that this last year we both salted and smoked our meat too hard. It is a touch too dry. Other years it has been superb. It beats bought stuff into a cocked hat. The only thing—you have to cut the bacon when you come down in the morning first thing (after you've had a cup of course—to have to do it before that would be inhuman) and then soak it in water until it is wanted for the frying pan. If any family ate as much bacon as we do, and had to buy it at current prices, it would cost them an awful lot of money.

The hams we are inclined to cut up like this too, and have fried ham and eggs for breakfast, but sometimes we will lop a ham in half and boil half of it and have some of it hot and the rest cold.

This all sounds a terrible labour and performance. And it is.

In fact when we kill a pig there is perhaps an afternoon's work on the day on which we kill it (killing, singeing and scraping, paunching and splitting it in half). The next day we are at it all day—and well into the night. And the next day too. And after that the odd hour or two of work. And, after the big operation, the living-room is like a butcher's shop, with fat all over the stove and the floor, bits of meat here and there, soup on the rug, and grease all over the cat and the children. It is no mean operation. But strangely enough it is fun. It is fun working at a big job flat out—when you can really see something at the end of it for your labours. And after all—the biggest part of the job is the canning, and when we do that we have the knowledge that we are doing our *cooking* for many days of the year ahead. Because when we open a can of pork there is hardly any cooking to do—just heat it up and eat it. So two days, we feel, are not wasted, when much of the next year's cooking is being completed on them.

There is not much food preserving necessary for some time after the winter pig-killing. Our neighbour Richard cans hares, but we have never got round to that. We get fresh hares all the year round anyway. But the early part of the year—from February right through to May—is the dreaded "hungry gap". It is what we preserve *for*. It is the time when people used to go down like flies from scurvy, and become like skin and bone. Whenever there is a surplus of milk, though, we make cheese; but that is generally in the summer. As it might happen at any time of the year though I will describe it at this point. Sally is making a washed curd cheese today—I just now had to leave my desk and go and help her lift the heavy pot off the stove.

We have a big aluminium open pot which holds four and a half gallons. Every day we throw surplus milk into that (after the cream has been skimmed off it for butter) and when it is full we put in on the stove until it is luke warm and then put cheese rennet in. It curdles, and we cut it into lovely little cubes with a knife, and then put it back on the stove. We let it warm very slowly then to a hundred degrees, take it off, drain the whey off (to go to the pigs of course) and plop the cubes of curd into a piece of muslin. When this has drained a bit we put it in the cheese press (which we bought in Norwich for half a crown— the shopkeeper didn't know what it was. All he knew was that he had it) and press it for a couple of days. We pull it out— bandage it with muslin and rub it with fat—and leave it for at least three weeks before we eat it.

If, however, the milk being stored up in the aluminium pot

goes thick by itself, we just turn this into cream cheese. This is simplicity itself—we plop it all into a piece of muslin and hang it up to drip. After it has dripped—lo—it is cream cheese. With bits of raw onion, carrots, parsley and other herbs, chopped up small and put in it, it is superb.

But hard cheese is the thing, for it enables us to carry over a surplus of milk to a time of scarcity. The stuff will keep for a long time, and the hungry gap is made less hungry.

There is not much food preserving in the summer—until the soft fruit comes along. And as very little came along this summer (owing to those dam' greenfly) there wasn't much then this year. But before there has always been a good harvest of black currants, and consequent jam boiling, and a harvest of gooseberries with consequent bottling as well as jam boiling. With the ever-eager Aga at hand this is not a laborious job.

Then come the runner beans. These are the great stand-by. We pick 'em young (no use waiting until they get old and stringy—that is the fatal mistake)—pick 'em as they come ready which means a picking every day, chop them up which we do with a little machine that we bought from the ironmonger's, put them down into a huge crock, and sprinkle dry salt on every layer of a couple of inches of beans. As the days go on the crock gets fuller, until it is quite full, when we put it away in the larder and give the rest of the runner beans away to the cow. Then, in the dark days of the winter, all we have to do when we want green vegetables is to fish out a handful of beans, soak in water for a couple of hours, and then cook. They are almost indistinguishable from new-picked beans.

After the beans the sweet corn begins to come along. This also we pick young, and the surplus beyond our daily requirements we boil, scrape the grain off the cobs with a knife, dry it on a wire gauze thing over the stove or in the slow oven, then put it away in tin canisters. In the hungry gap—soak for twelve hours—heat in water and eat. Nearly as good as new.

By then maybe the tomatoes are ripening. Drop into scalding water for a moment so that the skins come off, put into Kilner jars, top up with sugar and salt and spices, boil for an hour, screw up and leave. They give a life and a grace and vitality to food dishes right through the year.

Onions require nothing further than hanging up in strings (a delightful job for a sunny afternoon, by the front door) and keeping.

Potatoes we clamp by heaping them up on the ground, covering with straw and then earth, or else just heap them in the food-store and cover with sacks. Carrots we bury in the shed in light dry earth. Parsnips we don't lift until the dead of winter—and then just stack them in the shed. Marrows, squashes, pumpkins, we store on Sally's pottery racks in the big brick shed. They last until they go bad.

Every other year we have a huge haul of wild plums from some trees in Star-goose, and of these we make perhaps forty or fifty pounds of bottled plums. This year looks as if it is going to be a lean one for them—last year was bumper. We opened our last jar the other day.

Crab apples are marvellous, for nothing in the world touches crab-apple jelly. One year, when much else had failed, Sally and I were driving in the van to Nottingham of all places. Sally suddenly noticed a whole hedge of crab apple-trees. We always, when we had the van, carried some empty sacks in the back of it. We filled one of these right up, and had crab-apple jelly for a year and a day. Our own crab apple-trees are coming along nicely though, so we won't have to go to Nottingham.

Mushrooms we get in the autumn if we have the initiative to go and look for them on the marshes. These we eat fresh of course—but we dry a lot in the hot cupboard and they keep the winter through. This year we intend to try to make ketchup with them also.

Of haricot-type beans we have tried many varieties. We have found the best—some medium-sized brown beans that we brought from Holland—and these we pick ripe, hang to dry, thresh, and store and they last the year through.

Much of this food preserving we had to learn from books; so many of these are now available that they can easily be found in bookshops and local libraries.

To Preserve what we Produce

Wine is another great activity. And I suppose it is fitting that —as I drink most of it—I should do most of the work of preparing it.

The whole mystique of wine making was an apparently unfathomable mystery to me when we came here. Trying to follow recipes in a book one got a sense of complete illogicality. *Why* should one recipe call for four and a half ounces of this and three and a quarter of that? Was there some fearful mystery about it?

In fact of course it's all a lot of fiddle-faddle. The basic principle of wine making is this, and when you know it you can throw the recipe books away.

If you are lucky enough to live in a country in which grapes will grow you can make wine by crushing the grapes and allowing the juice to ferment. This is because grape juice (from properly ripened grapes) has enough sugar in it to turn into the right strength of alcohol, and the right yeast germs in it to ferment the sugar.

In England we have no fruit with enough sugar in it, and the yeasts we have are too unreliable. So what we do in fact is buy sugar from the grocers. We dissolve this in water, which we get from the tap, and ferment it into alcohol by putting yeast in it, which we buy from the baker, and letting it stand in a warm place.

Now I doubt whether just pure sugar and water would be sufficient substitute for yeast alone, and so we add some vegetable matter to it too. Also, the flavour of wine made from just sugar would be dull, and so we add a well-flavoured vegetable matter. In other words we take our fruit, or our flower, or our root or stem or leaf, and either boil it or soak it in water, add sugar, add yeast, and let it ferment. The sugar turns into alcohol. The flavour of the vegetable matter is retained, very strongly, in the wine.

While it is fermenting it is giving off carbonic acid gas, and provided you keep a clean towel or a piece of cloth over the top of the crock in which it is fermenting no enemy organisms can get in. After it has finished fermenting you have to cork it up securely, or foreign bugs—bacteria and yeasts—will get in and turn it into vinegar or make it go bad.

Since we have been here we have made wine of cowslips, parsnips, elder-berries, crab apple, wheat, marrow, broom flowers, grapes and sloes.

The cowslip was superb, but never since that first year have we had enough cowslips. The crab apple was unfortunate. Firstly, the apples probably have quite a lot of native sugar in them and so we should not have added so much. Secondly I added what we decided to add without telling Sally—and *she* then came along and added the same amount again!

The yeast cannot turn all that amount of sugar into alcohol —because when the alcohol gets to a certain strength it kills the yeast. So the stuff tasted like very sickly alcoholic grenadine. It was revolting and we gave it to the pigs which made them as drunk as people.

Knowing what we now know we would not have given the pigs that treat. We would have tried refermenting it, mixing it first with another load of vegetable matter—added some lemons perhaps—anything the flavour of which would not have clashed with the apples and which would have given more non-sugar matter for the yeast to work. Then we might have corked the stuff up in bottles and tied the corks and let it finish its fermenting in the bottle to make a kind of "champagne". The fun of wine making is to try different things.

Wheat wine is a swizz, because you have to buy the wheat and buy a great quantity of raisins which you have to put with it. Just what the wheat contributes I have never been able to find out. Anyway I have a gallon maturing away in a sealed stone bottle on top of the dresser for next Christmas.

Elder-berry wine is heady stuff, and perhaps a bit sickly; but it has stood us in good stead. Last year I tried the experiment of not adding any water to it, but expressing the pure juice of the berries by putting a vast quantity of them through the mangle. The resulting liquor is thick, strong-tasting, and drunk-making. It is fine if you treat it as a liqueur; but if you gollop it down don't blame me if it makes you sick. Elder flower—alas

—we have always been too busy in the season to make any; but I have drunk other people's and it is perhaps the best of the lot. "Elder flower champagne" can be as delicate as any imported wine. If the Greeks and the Romans had lived in a climate where the elder grew but no grapes—the wine-snobs of this world would scoff at "home-made grape wine", and talk a lot of nonsense about "the miraculous juice of the elder".

But Broom flower is our speciality, as it should be at a place called the Broom. In fact we gave a bottle to a neighbour this year and his daughter put it in the flower show and it won second prize. The judges said that if it hadn't been for "the presentation" it would have won first, for it was the best wine they had ever tasted.

Every year we pick a huge basket full of the flowers (the stuff grows in great profusion in the Warren), put them in a pillow slip, boil them in water in the copper, pull them out, scoop the water into a big crock (about eight gallons), add sugar, wait until it is cool enough not to kill the yeast and add yeast, chuck in a few lemons (flowers by themselves need acid), cover with a cloth and let it hubble away for three weeks. Then carefully we "rack" (syphon) it out into a number of crocks with small necks, put cotton-wool in the necks and let them stand another few weeks. This is in case any more gas is to come off—this year we corked some up securely and got a kind of "champagne", or bubbly. Then we rack again into bottles— leave to mature as long as we can (nine months is the longest we have managed) and the result is a perfectly clear, light greeny yellow, rather too sweet, delicately flavoured, wine, one wineglass of which will make your head begin to go round. I have never met anyone yet who did not think that it was delicious. There is one small point I must add—one should not put acid things in a copper, or it spoils the wine.

It is our aim to try many more materials, find the ones which suit us the best, and gradually build up a big stock of bottles. We have a lot of thirsty friends and need an awful *lot* of wine. It is no good our messing about with a gallon of this and a gallon of that. Eight gallons at a time is a good round quantity

—and even that goes long before it is mature. We must try to make it faster than we can drink it, so as to build up a stock. The light flower wines we find you can drink pretty young: the heavier red wines need a year or two in the bottle. Maturing in the wood would be better, but barrels are expensive. And next year—perhaps this year if the sun will only come out a little—we will start experimenting with grapes. I have tasted white wine made from English-grown grapes and it tasted like a very fine hock. For the more northerly the climate, the smaller will be the yield of grapes that you will get from your vines, but the more delicate the flavour of your wine. Champagne does not come from Italy. The Rhine has a colder climate than Suffolk.

As for the cost of home-made wine—a bottle costs fourpence. That is the cost of the sugar. The yeast is infinitesimal, and we already have the bottles because in the days before we made our own wine we used to buy a lot of imported.

Last summer I kept a "ginger beer plant" going, and turned out an awful lot of ginger beer. But I gave it up in the end. My heart was not in it. If this was a country with sensible laws I should distil brandy. It is not, but I must just describe a simple still that I have seen operating in Himachayall Pradesh, a hill state in India. It is so simple, and so safe.

A large vessel full of wine or beer over a slow fire. A smaller vessel inside it floating on the wine or beer. A largest of all vessel balanced on top of the first large vessel—so that it covers it and overspreads its top. Cold water running into the largest of all vessel on top—and pouring over the side by a spout.

What happens? The alcohol in the wine or beer boils off—hits the under side of the widest-of-all vessel, which is cold because of the water, condenses on it, and drips down into the small floating vessel. Provided you do not go on with the process too long you will have a distilled spirit in the small floating vessel. If the police suddenly arrive? You will have a large vessel full of wine or beer, which is quite legal. You will have an even larger empty vessel which may be used for boiling the nappies in. You will have a smaller vessel, upside down on the floor. Still? Where? Still indeed.

To Preserve what we Produce

A word on herrings. This year, in default of catching a respectable number, we bought three hundred from Lowestoft, *via* a local fish merchant, for twopence each. One can only get them at this price for a few weeks of course, and then they are far and away the best value in high protein that you can buy. We spent a late evening heading them, splitting them down the belly, cleaning them, scraping off all the scales (troublesome but well worth it), and packing them down in two crocks in dry salt. Plenty of salt—for you cannot have too much.

Now, from time to time, we pull out a dozen or two, soak them for twenty-four hours in fresh water, eat a few raw (what the Dutch buy from barrows at every street corner), bone the rest by laying them flat on their tummies—pressing hard along the ridge of their backs, then pulling out the backbones. We then roll each boned herring around a piece of onion, stick a sharpened matchstick through it, and pop it in a jar which we fill with vinegar and spices. In a fortnight we have rollmops fit for a king.

9

The Raft-Loads

Robinson Crusoe was supplied with several large raft loads of gear from the wreck of the ship. He had a very great deal of what it takes to live in the wilderness, and he did not have to pay for it. And Defoe showed a sound insight into the sort of things that he would require.

We left *our* ship (fortunately not quite a wreck) bringing away practically no gear at all. True we did salvage a hundred and twenty fathoms of two-and-a-half inch Italian hemp rope, which was too big for her running rigging but which we had come by as a bit of a windfall, and also a little paint, and a few odd tools, shackles, and things like that. But we did not rob the ship when we left her: we left her with a full complement of boatswain's stores.

But we were so ill-provided when we went to the Broom that, before we could grow so much as a cabbage, we had to buy a spade.

Now a spade costs thirty bob.

And little by little we found ourselves forced into buying a whole great armoury of tools.

Tools that I do not think that we could well live without here are:

An axe.
A spade.
A mattock (for paring-off turf, or for use as a pick).
A scythe.

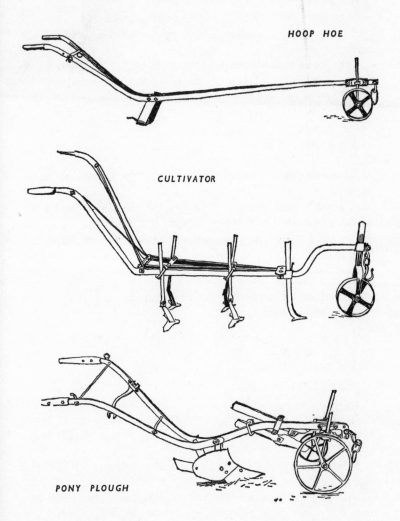

HOOP HOE

CULTIVATOR

PONY PLOUGH

The Raft-Loads

A rubber (for sharpening the scythe).

A bagging-hook (sickle-shaped cutting tool).

A long-handled slasher (like a billhook—for cutting back hedges).

Two forks (one a potato-lifting fork with wide tines. Four-pronged forks are inferior devices. Five tines are best.)

A "bushman" saw.

Three hoes.

An iron rake.

A wooden hay rake.

Two pitch forks.

A croom (long-handled fork with tines turned at right-angles).

A wheelbarrow (ours is a poor tool—we really need a big wooden one with rubber tyre but cannot afford it).

A lawn mower—now not needed as Pinto mows it for us.

A trowel.

Pair of secateurs.

With these we can scratch the land. But after we got the horse we acquired—generally for nominal prices:

Two ploughs (one would be enough—but we got one and then saw a better).

Pair of heavy barrows (he will just pull one section).

Pair of light harrows.

Hoop hoe.

Inter-row cultivator (the most useful tool we have got. It has ten tines and can expand sideways to adjust to different width rows).

Steerage horse hoe (never got round to using it yet. Will one day though).

Van (recently acquired for a fiver. A beautiful little builder's van with varnished sides, elegantly shaped, exquisitely built. We intend it for carting muck but it is really too big for Pinto. We'll either have to get a smaller vehicle or a bigger horse).

What we urgently require is one section of a spring-tine

116

harrow—the sort of thing that you see being drawn in a large gang behind a tractor. The experience of other people shows that this is the ideal tool for obtaining a seed bed with a horse. We also would like, if we could find them, a "double tom" or ridging plough and—very hard to find—a miniature mowing machine. One can buy a multi-purpose plough—ridging or ploughing—from Planet Tools, new, but we cannot afford to buy new horse tools when the junk yards of this country are piled high with good old ones. The trouble though, is finding them.

Other refinements that we have added to our outdoor armoury are:

A hand spray for fruit trees.

A "Jalo" wheel hoe, with "ploughing", ridging, harrowing, attachments.

A "Jalo" seeder.

Another seeder which selects the seed by means of notches on a rubber band, and is very good indeed; but cannot be used for anything as big as beet seed.

Then, because every job that is done at the Broom has to be done by ourselves we found ourselves forced to build up, little by little, a complete workshop: carpenters' tools, iron-working tools, spanners, stilsons, sledge-hammer, beetle (big wooden mallet), a big stock of nails, screws, bolts, staples, and wood. A plane is expensive—but it is far more expensive to employ a carpenter. We have tools to do carpentry, bricklaying, plumbing, glazing, concreting, painting, plastering, papering, fence making, tree felling, wood sawing: to mention just a few of the activities that we have had to engage in.

All this has been very expensive. In the days when we still had the van every time that we went to town we would come back with some more expensive tools, or coils of wire, tins of paint, bags of cement, wire netting, odds and ends of all sorts.

Most of the people whom I know who have converted old cottages, and established new homes in old houses, have had several hundred pounds with which to pay a firm of contractors to do it for them. We had nothing but an overdraft, and had to do it all ourselves, and also, because of our remoteness, contractors charge us too much. But the buying of the tools and equipment was a great strain on our economy. As fast as we could earn money—which was not very fast—it went out again on expensive equipment.

We have the equipment now. We can live here for the rest of our lives, and cope with any task which presents itself, and never have the great outlay again.

I do not think that most people moving to the country would have quite such a big outlay to make. For most people at least start with something. Nearly everyone has a spade. And a hammer. We, having lived afloat, had nothing: for we left what we did have aboard the boat.

Then the kitchen, buttery, winery, stillroom, and the rest of it called for a complete equipment as well.

I do not see how one could live as we do without at least, say, five big crocks. They cost about thirty shillings each. Then big stoneware basins to let the cream settle in. If you have a cow you need a stool to sit on while you milk her and a bucket to milk her into. If you make cheese you need a very big pot for heating the milk in, a cheese press (we made a cake tin do with a lot of bricks piled on top of it at first, but it was time-wasting. We eventually bought a cheese press from a man who didn't know what it was, see page 106). If you make wine you need big stoneware bottles or flasks (we were lucky in finding a number of two and one-gallon ones for a few bob at a cottage break-up. I have just ordered a four-gallon taphole jar from Loftus, 24 Tottenham Road, London W.1., for two guineas. Something must have rushed to my head). We recently got a corking-machine and it has proved well worth its price.

We needed a great battery of Kilner jars, big canisters for storing dry foods like dried sweet corn, haricot beans. A big sterilizer for bottling fruit, a thermometer. Bread tins for baking bread, a big bowl for the dough to rise in. The canning machine and plenty of empty tins.

A kitchen that is used as ours is: as a food factory, bake

office, cannery, butchery, grocery, winery, dairy, has to be lavishly equipped.

No doubt all this equipment has already paid for itself, in saving us having to spend more money on food already prepared. After all—if you have to buy tinned food you really do find yourself delving into your pocket. Our tinning machine cost us a fiver, but I could balance all the money that we have spent on tinned foods in the last three years on my nose. Many a family spends a fiver a week on food—we eat very well for many a week without spending more than a few pennies.

And we still *have* the equipment, and much of it will last our lives out and our children's lives too. It is the sort of equipment which, in a civilized and settled society, a man and a woman inherit from their parents.

There are still a very few things that we need for the house. More stoneware jars and bottles for making and maturing wine. Or a few wooden casks would be very nice. A large stainless steel pot to go on the Aga for the large-scale boiling of jams, or sterilizing of tins. Such things would save time— and time is important.

We got a lot of what we needed very cheaply.

We attended sales at a small local market, and often bought up a job-lot from some cottage break-up which had in it numbers of odd things which would have cost us fifty times as much had we gone to a shop and bought them new. But time spent in going to sales is grudged: there is so much that you could be doing at home.

Often, when I fight my way through our overcrowded and I fear often untidy kitchen, I wonder why we need such an awful amount of apparatus just in order to live.

In the Army I lived for years, quite happily, with two halves of a mess tin, a knife, a fork, a spoon, and an enamelled mug. I love simplicity, and scarcity of possessions. I envy the *sadhu* whose sole possessions are a begging bowl, a rosary, and a rag round his middle. How unlike a *sadhu* we are at the Broom.

But the simple life, alas, once you really try to lead it, leads you into all this complication! You cannot live, and rear a family, on your own little share of your country, growing your own food, preserving and processing it, without this vast assemblage of tools and implements. In a peasant society presumably the peasant inherits at least some of this apparatus from his forebears.

Thoreau lived at Walden with very little apparatus indeed, and grew all his own food. He gives a very complete list of his belongings, and a complete balance-sheet of his financial transactions. But he only lived there for two years. And he had no family. He was prepared to live almost exclusively on beans. Try to persuade a five-and-a-half-year-old daughter who is just beginning to go to the village school, to live exclusively on beans! And we live hard and work hard here—on most days both Sally and I cram sixteen hours of work into the day: double what is normal nowadays. And half of this in the open air. I do not believe that we could do this on just beans. I sometimes consider though—that if we did not demand such good food we would not have to work so hard—and therefore would not *need* so much good food! Thoreau did nothing most of the day but just sit around and think. He did not require much food. If I were a bachelor I should want to do just that. I think that his was the perfect mode of existence—for a bachelor. But surely a mode of existence must be worked out that does not entail every man being a bachelor. But here one gets into very deep philosophical waters.

At any rate—we *have* all this apparatus now, and no longer do we have to make constant journeys into town to buy five or ten or fifteen pounds' worth of tools and implements.

And just as we have already got most of our capital equipment, so we have done, I hope, the greater part of what I call our "capital work". To dig a piece of land is not "capital work", it is routine, recurring work. But yesterday afternoon and the afternoon before that I spent my time digging and laying an underground drain, from what used to be a small lake in our yard every time it rained, to the fence into Stargoose. The lake has now disappeared, and henceforth we will be able to walk to the food store, or Goose Bit, or the shed, or the cow shed, without putting our rubber boots on.

This I call "capital work". Work that will not have to be done again. Work at making a permanent improvement, that will make our routine work less, or pleasanter, or more productive.

Most of the work that we have done since we came here comes under that heading, and we have had to do the "routine work" alongside it. There is still a lot of "capital work" to do. But when the last of it is done, then our lives will be very much easier. For, not only will we not have to earn so much money by trading with the outside world to buy capital equipment, but we will not have to do so much "capital work" at home. We will be able to concentrate on growing our food, processing it, making many of the artifacts which we require and would otherwise have to buy from outside, doing a little work for money, and lying in the sun. We have not done half enough of *that* these last few years. Although—and it might seem strange to anyone who has read thus far in this book— we have done some. More than the reader might suppose.

A few more items of capital equipment might save us an awful lot of labour out of doors. A self-feeder for the pigs for example, and also one for the hens. One of those large galvanized-iron bins which you can put a hundredweight of dry food into and then just leave it alone for a week or two, while the animals or birds help themselves. With these devices, and "lidos" as we call them—ramps cut out of the edge of the field to allow animals access to the water in the ditch—we could leave the place for a week at a time unattended.

An electric fence might, or might not, be a good idea. Michael lent us one once, and it was always going wrong. Some people have an absolute positive effect on mechanical devices which makes them go wrong, and I am one of them. I only have to *look* at an electrical or mechanical device and it goes wrong. But it takes me a precious afternoon to erect a fence of pig-netting. I could do the same area with an electric fence in ten minutes. But then I would have to slog up to the village every so often to get the batteries recharged. This fencing difficulty will gradually resolve itself, however. For every time now that I erect a fence *across* my field—I leave it there. The field will soon be cut up, therefore, into a number of narrow sectors, and it will be a simple job to fold stock across any one of these sectors by erecting one straight fence across the sector, and another perhaps behind the stock; or alternatively just to graze each sector as a whole. The pros and cons of an electric fence are many and various. An electric fence will not stop small pigs. It is difficult to make it stop sheep, and we intend to have sheep. I rather doubt whether it would stop geese.

I sometimes wonder though—is all this equipment really necessary?

Supposing we really were Robinson Crusoes—could we not get along with very much less equipment than we have got?

Well, the answer is that of course we could. But then we would have to live in a much more simple fashion.

If we lived on very simple food: bread and potatoes, milk and butter, beans, salt pork and bacon, chicken and eggs, and the simplest of vegetables and only in their season: then we could do without many tools and much apparatus and also save a lot of work. But we would have to do without wine, without jams and pickles, tinned pork and brawn, bottled tomatoes and fruit and many other things.

Robinson Crusoe lived quite happily in a cave and a hut. He did not worry about embellishing the walls. He was one of the most severely practical men who have ever been invented. I imagine that he did not add one single piece of decoration, embellishment, or pattern, to his dwelling or his belongings.

Sally is now painting a mermaid on the side of the bath.

I am quite sure that Robinson Crusoe managed to get along very well without either a mermaid or a bath.

I am busy, after "work" in the evenings, running off a thousand wine labels on the printing press. Our wine would taste just as good without elaborately printed labels—or would it? We could do quite well without wine—or could we? Living is not just a battle to survive and no more. Crusoe had little time for anything but survival (and his rather extraordinary effort to turn Friday into a Christian—extraordinary because one feels that the arguments he brought forward to *support* Christianity would in fact have put a cannibal—or anyone else for that matter—against it). I suppose it is all a matter of balance—what you are prepared to pay for what. If you want mermaids painted on the side of your bath then you have got to work rather harder than otherwise in order to paint them, to earn money to buy the paint, the brushes, and the bath. We are prepared to go to some trouble to have bright and good patterns about us, Sally's beautiful pottery, brightly painted walls, things pleasing to the eye. And things pleasing to the palate too. Alas—our flower garden is a thing still in our imaginations. This year we do intend to get to work on it. But there are wild flowers, and blossoms on the wild plum trees, and the beautiful woods and marshes, and the cries of the marsh birds coming to us at night as we lie in bed, and the song of the nightingales in the summer time—

The Blackbirds and the Thrushes sing on every green tree,
And the Larks they sing melodious at the Dawning of the Day.

—as they sing in our local pub.

So we are not altogether bereft of beauty. But natural beauty is not enough. There must also be plenty of that different sort of beauty which is created, consciously, by man.

I have no doubt that if we had a week or two to prepare for it we could live here at the Broom, on our five acres and with the wild food from the surrounding woods, estuaries and marshes, for the rest of our lives without any contact with the rest of the world at all. That is if the rest of the world would leave us alone, which it would not. But by doing so we would lose a great deal. Society is good as well as bad, and we have no objection to trading in a controlled way with the rest of the world.

But living here, so far away from society, has altered our sense of values. We find that we no longer place the same importance on artifacts and gadgets as other people do. Also—

every time we buy some factory-made article—we wonder what sort of people made it—if they enjoyed making it or if it was just a bore—what sort of life the maker, or makers, lead. Every time I have to travel to other places—to London or Birmingham—I wonder where all the activity I see in those places is leading. Is it really leading to a better or richer or simpler life for people? Or not? Whenever the Yankee planes roar over my head, as they do many times a day because we have an air base near here, I wonder about the nature of "progress". One can progress in so many different directions. Up a gum-tree for example.

I know that the modern Birmingham factory worker is supposed to lead an "easier" life than, say, a French peasant. But I wonder if this supposition is correct. And I wonder if, whether "easier" or not, it is a better life? Simpler? Healthier? More spiritually satisfying? Or not?

I don't wonder very long. I have pretty well made my own mind up about it. And every time we buy a plastic cup from Woolworth's (fortunately not very often because Sally makes her own cups) we feel that we are condoning, subscribing to, a certain way of life of which we do not approve. And we are condoning, and subscribing to, the jet planes that roar overhead making the day hideous and scrawling their snail-slime over our lovely Suffolk sky.

So we buy as far as possible from other "cranks".

We get our cloth from a hand-weaver, who lives at Lavenham. His cloth is made without benefit of any Yorkshire slums —or barrack-like housing estates either. He lives in a pleasant cottage, like we do. He works in his own time, to please himself. He charges rather less than Big Industry for his cloth—and his cloth is rather better. (His name is Jarvis, in case anyone is interested.)

As far as we can we import our needs from small and honest craftsmen and tradesmen. We subscribe as little as we can to the tycoons, and the Ad-men, and the boys with the expense accounts. If we could subscribe nothing at all we would be the better pleased.

10

Wild Food

There is a weed called fat hen which worries farmers very much in this country. In that time of the year when we are tired of eating asparagus, but when other summer vegetables have not yet come on, fat hen is our main green dish. Cut when it is young and succulent and lightly boiled it is like a very much nicer spinach.

The other day I brought home a basket of samphire from the saltings in our local estuary. This is a fleshy leaved seaweed which tastes delicious either boiled or pickled. We have never had enough of it yet to pickle it—to get sufficient for this would mean half a day going down the estuary in a boat, and that we have not had time to do. I have often tasted it pickled up near the shores of the Wash, where it is a national dish. But used as a vegetable it is quite unlike anything else, and I know of very few things which I would rather eat.

I have mentioned mushrooms. Last year they were few because it was too dry—this year they are few because it was too wet. The marshes in which we used to find them have been practically under water. Wild mushrooms are becoming a very scarce bird in this country. This is due to the use of chemicals on the land, the lack of horses, and probably most of all to the periodic ploughing up of pastures and cropping and reseeding. The beneficent mycelium does not have time to establish itself. We are going to try, this March, to enspore our own piece of permanent pasture. The mushrooms grown on compost in sheds or dark cellars taste as much like real mushrooms as margarine tastes like butter.

We have recently been trying several kinds of edible toadstools. Some, I might say, are more edible than others. We tried a thing called the "oyster mushroom" the other day—a growth on dead trees—and it took half the morning to get the little wriggling black-headed white maggots out of the fins of it. Not a diet for the squeamish—and then it didn't taste up to much. But giant puff ball is the easiest food in the world to prepare, for it cuts cleanly into lovely firm white slices which can be fried in butter; and then it is delicious. Parasol mushroom is another favourite of ours. It tastes similar to field mushroom but is stronger flavoured and I think better. Champignon, or "fairy ring", toadstools are fine if you can find enough of them to make it worth cooking them, for they go down, as cooks say, "to nothing". Bluetts (a large toadstool) we get along the borders of the pine woods, and they are good eating.

Watercress is found in plenty in the dikes in the marshes, and, besides being good as a salad, it makes a fine soup, boiled, and then pressed through the *moule*.

Our ditches also yield eels.

We had a good source of eels once from a great floating pump which a neighbour installed in the "delft" (the wide ditch behind the sea wall). This machine used to get blocked from time to time by a large fat eel, and the electric pump would "trip out", and the man whose job it was to trip it in again was a friend of ours and he used to bring us the eels. We could easily get more eels by going and catching them. An "eel hive" would be a desirable adjunct to the next "raft load" that we bring ashore—this is a wicker-work trap which one baits with fresh fish and drops into the water. The eels swim in and can't swim out again. Everyone round about here though used to use "pritches", or eel-tridents, to stab the mud of the ditches to spear eels. Nowadays, if they eat eels at all, they would buy them from Holland, via Billingsgate. They neglect the good food under their noses.

Wild Food

For a fat eel, cooked anyhow, is delicious. And smoked—I doubt if the flesh can experience a fiercer pleasure than that of eating smoked eels.

If we were not so near the salt water estuary and the sea, we would think much more about freshwater fish. Foods go by fashions. At present it is the fashion "not to like" freshwater fish. They are supposed to "taste muddy". Just as wigeon (a kind of wild duck) are supposed to taste "fishy". This faddiness about food is something, in my opinion, to be deplored, and if it exists in oneself to be ashamed of. *Anybody* (except perhaps a diabetic) can eat—and *enjoy*—anything that anybody else can eat and enjoy. If only he approaches it without prejudice and with an open mind. We have tried roach, and pike. To my mind few fish are nicer than a pike. In Isaac Walton's day these things were considered delicacies. What has changed—the pike or the palates? Simply fashion—that is all.

People round about here used to rear their families on hares. Now they turn up their noses at them and won't eat them at any price. This is snobbery. Hare used to be the food of a man who could afford nothing else—now, in the lollipop state, when we can afford fish and chips (albeit that the fish has been dead for a month and is probably mud shark and the chips have been fried in some unmentionable "vegetable oil") why should we eat hare? In spite of the fact that hare is one of the finest delicacies that there is. There is one slight disadvantage to hare though and that is that skinning and cleaning one is a messy job. But it is not as bad as all that. It is simply one of those jobs that one gets on with, does without thinking too much about it, and that is that. You have good meat for a couple of days—and meat for the dog (who in our case probably caught it).

Pheasants we are not allowed to shoot, for this is not our land. The landlord, as is usual, retains the right to take game. This is illogical and absurd, for the hirer of land should be entitled to the produce of the land and wild game is part of that. It is one of the laws or customs that derive from the fact of England being a conquered country. But if a man owned five acres he would be well advised to encourage the pheasants, and shoot them sparingly, and make use of this excellent source of very good food. To the tenant—they are just an unmitigated nuisance. I cannot persuade the people in the village here that I do not poach my landlord's pheasants. They all believe that anyone—living where I do surrounded by these birds—must naturally live on them. The other day I went into the King's Head and a man said: "We're just getting a sweepstake up on your behalf, John."

"Why?" I asked.

"To raise some cash to buy you a brace of pheasants for Christmas."

And there was a hideous guffaw of laughter all round. I cannot persuade them of what is the truth: that if I *did* poach pheasants it would not be on my landlord's land. There are plenty of other landlords. In any case, I never manage to eat through our chickens and ducks to get them down to a reasonable number.

Of wild fruits we always make a harvest of anything that is going, almost on principle. It seems to us to be blasphemous to refuse these gifts. Elder-berries not only make wine—they make fine jam, with a taste and a tang unlike anything else. Blackberries go without saying. Wild plums and bullaces we are well supplied with near the house, although they come and go in seasons—this year was a poor one for wild plums although magnificent for other fruit. There is a green lane, very much overgrown, and still—in spite of "myxy"—full of rabbits, and it is lined with sloe bushes. There, this year, we picked enough of the most large and luxurious sloes that I have seen to make five gallons of sloe wine. (You do *not* need to put gin into sloe wine—water, sugar, and yeast are all that is needed.) Last year I followed a recipe I saw in a book for making rose hip syrup of the kind that you can get from the "National Health" for children. It made a delicious drink, a little going a long way in water. Alas, this year it got forgotten and it is now already too late.

In the pine wood there are pigeons for the plonking, but with twelve-bore cartridges sevenpence each they are an expensive food. Sally, however, is an adept at shooting them from the bedroom window with the .22 (cartridges a halfpenny each). Wild fowl—wigeon and mallard, teal, curlew and other birds—come to our estuary in thousands, but I seldom have time to go and shoot any. As a bachelor I did a lot of fowling, but now it is just impossible to spare the time to spy out the grounds, observe the lines of flight, go night after night perhaps for nothing, just for another article of diet. It is easier to wring a tame bird's neck. Although no tame duck, to my mind, can equal the taste of a pair of young wigeon, well hung, roasted, and eaten with fried bread crumbs and some slices of orange. One day, when all the "capital work" is finished, perhaps I shall get down to the estuaries again.

The salt water does provide us with good food though.

Our neighbour Richard has a motor fishing-boat, and spends a lot of his time fishing. He also has an oyster farm in the estuary. Sometimes I help him fish, or work his oysters, and get either fish or oysters for my pains. With a little otter trawl he

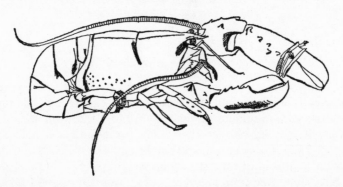

gets "flats": soles, plaice, dabs, flounders, and "roka" or skate, codling and lobsters. With drift nets we managed to get a few herring this year, but herring are leaving the North Sea. The continental herring trawlers are taking them away—big, little, and even eggs—to dump into the maws of the fish-meal factories. As men become better at catching fish it stands to reason that there will be fewer fish. There are progressively fewer herring in the North Sea.

Sea trout, or salmon trout (exactly like salmon excepting for some minor differences) come along this coast every summer, and we spend several nights out in a small boat off the breakers, fishing for them with a seine, or "draw net". The biggest one we caught last summer was eight and a half pounds. Fresh they are delicious: smoked they are a delight.

Richard also gets sprats: fine fresh or smoked (any oily fish, or fat flesh or fowl, is apt to be good smoked). Shrimps can be caught right in the estuary. Mullet swim up the rivers in thousands, but are hard to catch because they jump the nets. A trammel, I believe, would do them. Unpopular with local people, they are one of the nicest fish that you can catch. Richard and I have sometimes discussed building an old-fashioned "fish weir". That is a permanent fence in the estuary that would entrap fish. This would provide a regular supply of fresh fish for very little labour, and whatever the weather:

> *Wind from the Nor-thard, Wind from the East,*
> *Many a haul but never a Feast.*
> *Swell the net full!*
> *Swell the net full!*
> *Weir fish for Wednesday swell the net full!*

Along the low-tide mark in our estuary is a thick line of mussels—just half a mile from our house. These want cooking for the very minimum of time—put into a saucepan with no water in, the lid on, and over a hot flame until the shells all open. Then you can eat them straight away, or else with a wine sauce. People in this parish buy mussels in jars for four and six a jar. They come from Holland, and are not half as good as the ones we can get, by the bushel, for nothing.

But collecting wild food, whether from the fresh or salt water, the fields or the woods, or the air, takes time; and we do not do as much of it as we would like to. It is, however, part of our pleasure. If we go for a country walk, we keep our eyes open for fungi. When we used to have the van we always carried a sack or two in the back, for anything that looked edible and didn't belong to anybody. Chestnuts for example. Or crab apples. And a day's or a night's fishing is a relaxation: one must get away from the spade or the plough or the typewriter sometimes, and if one's pleasure leads to good food—how useful. We find that we have time for more fishing, fowling, and collecting, as time goes on.

But we shall never be able to live entirely without the spade or the milking bucket.

II

The Horse

W e bought the cow because we got tired of walking a couple of miles to fetch milk. We bought the pigs to help drink all the milk the cow gave. We increased our garden to feed the cow and to feed the pigs and to use up the incredible amount of manure which came from these animals. And I could see myself condemned for the rest of my days to hard labour with a spade. And so we bought the horse.

I read a lot of advertisements for those little garden tractors. Then I went and looked at several. But I found that to get one to do any real work at all would cost over a hundred pounds: anything smaller would just scrabble over the ground like a dog.digging for a bone. Further they make a terrible noise, and I like to hear the birds singing while I work. I think that is very important.

Then I met a smallholder who kept a horse to do his cultivating for him. What, we wondered, was wrong with a horse?

Well what is wrong with it? It will plough, cultivate, harrow, roll, horse-hoe: very much faster than a garden tractor costing a hundred pounds. It will do it silently without drowning the song of the birds. It will do it on grass, which is cheap and does not entail the expenditure of foreign currency. (Yes, a horse will work on grass—and grass alone. If you don't give him too much work to do.) You can ride a horse, and teach your children to ride, and you can make him pull a cart and take you to the pub when you want to go. And bring you back again, which is more important. He knows the way.

We wrote to an old friend of ours who lives in the Yorkshire Dales country, and asked him to keep his eye open for a Fell pony.

Keep his eyes open! He wired us next day to say he had bought her for us. And the next thing we knew was that I had to cadge a lift into the station—eight miles away—and walk back leading a horse.

Fanny was not a Fell pony, although no doubt she had Fell blood in her. She was more of a heavy Dales type. She was like a miniature cart horse, with heavy feathering on her legs. She cost £65, she had a saddle with her which cost a further six, and railage was £12 from farthest Yorkshire.

She was a sweet old thing. There was only one thing wrong with her. She was chronically and permanently lame. She had a disease called ring-bone, which is quite incurable. We could not use her on the road at all, and even to use her around the place was cruel.

We could see that she was lame, but knowing nothing about ring-bone thought it was something temporary. We had already bought a governess-cart—one of those staid black-painted vehicles with a box body in which the squire's children used to be taken out for healthful fresh air by their beloved governess —and we put Fanny into this and drove her into the nearest town: twelve miles away. We took her to a farrier there to have her shod, and it was he who told us that she had ring-bone.

I left her there the night, and went back to fetch her in the morning. It was then that I received the news she had ring-bone. I had nothing to do but to drive her back again. After all, ring-bone or no, I could not just *leave* her there. I suppose I could have sold her straight away to the cat's meat man.

So I put her in again and started the long way home. She was game enough. Without any encouragement from me she trotted along manfully, just nodding her head at every other step to show that she was lame.

I had not gone far when a woman in a car drove up alongside me and leaning out of window shrilled: "Your horse is lame!"

"I know she is, Madam," I replied. If I had been a ruder man I could have thought of several other things to say. She pulled her head in and drove off at high speed without saying another word.

But very shortly afterwards a police car drew alongside me, and I have never seen another police car on our deserted road before. "Your horse is lame," said the policeman.

"I know she is, Officer," I said.

"Well—what are you going to do about it?"

"Drive her home—what else can I do?"

"Where is your home?"

I told him. Another seven miles.

"You can't drive her in that condition," he said.

"All right then," I said. I was just beginning to tire of the discussion. "You know all about it—*you tell me what to do!*"

All this conversation was conducted with me trotting along gently, Fanny nodding her head, and the police car keeping pace alongside.

There was a silence. Then the policeman said: "Well, I don't see what you can do."

The Horse

"I don't either," I said. And I kept on trotting.

"I suppose you'd better just keep going," said the policeman.

"I suppose I had," I said.

And I kept on going. And the police car just drove away along the road, and shortly afterwards passed me going back the way it had come.

What is it about a certain kind of Englishwoman that makes her—at the sight of a horse—reach for the telephone? And telephone the police. They suddenly become emotional and irrational at the sight of a horse, or at the very idea of a horse. They never mind condemning a horse to *death*. They love to go about the country forcing people to send their horses to the knackers. If I could have asked Fanny—"would you rather I continue to drive you lame—or would you rather a man came and knocked you down and hung you up?" what would have been her answer? But these earnest Englishwomen have one answer to any problem concerning animals: "Have it put to sleep!" Maybe if they said: "Kill it!" instead of this sickly euphemism, they might have other ideas.

If we had had enough grass we would have kept Fanny, in spite of all the female humanitarian fuddy-duddies in the country, and worked her gently at the plough and the harrow, and bred a foal or two out of her. Because she was a lovely pony. Crossed with a thoroughbred she would have produced a hunter. And this plan would have pleased her better than the "humanitarian" answer to her problems. Being "put to sleep".

But we could not afford it. We intended to sell our van, and therefore it was essential that we had a road-going horse. We had only enough grass to keep one horse. So we wrote to our friend in the north.

He was horrified. He had bought Fanny from a friend, who had himself not seen her for months, for she had been running wild up on the moors. The man had sold the mare to him in good faith, for they both knew the mare well, and neither seller nor buyer knew of the fault. The man would replace the horse immediately, and my friend would send his son down with a new pony in a horse-box and take the old one away.

The Horse

Young George, and his young wife, accordingly turned up one evening in a Landrover, pulling a horse-box trailer behind with Pinto inside it.

And here is a tale which illustrates rather finely the state which English rural hospitality has got into.

Seven miles outside of King's Lynn, on the Sutton Bridge road, a wheel came off the horse-box. Luckily the pony was not damaged, and George and his wife managed to get him out. It was by then nine o'clock in the evening. They were stranded, with a horse, strangers in a strange land.

They walked, leading Pinto, the seven miles into King's Lynn. They asked at every farm they came to, and every large house, whether they could leave the pony there for the night. They did not want a stable. A tree to tie him to, in a safe place, would have been enough. They were both very young, and very likeable. It must have been obvious to everybody that their story was true, and that they were in one hell of a predicament. *Not one single person would help them.* George had one nice touch. When describing how one gentleman farmer had come to the door to speak to them—after they had trudged five miles and were just about at their wit's end—he imitated the emasculated south of England genteel accent to tell us how he heard the man's wife say: "Harold! Your coffee's getting cold dulling!"

At twelve o'clock at night they got into King's Lynn, met a rough old potato merchant who came to *them* and asked them if they were in trouble, and who stabled Pinto for them, found them a bed at a friend's, and lent them his own horse-box in the morning to continue their journey in. *And* refused to take any payment for it.

Noblesse oblige.

Anyway, Pinto arrived. A seven-year-old skewbald gelding, a very small cob I suppose: broad chested and stocky and very strong. And poor Fanny was taken away, to go where all the humanitarian ladies would have liked to have sent her.

All of which seems to me to say a lot for Yorkshire honesty and straight dealing.

The Horse

Pinto was full of life, a bit mischievous, loved the governess-cart, was used to the saddle and in spite of his size could carry me at least at a trot, but had never worked in chains.

We bought an old iron pony plough from the estate of a smallholder who had just died—one of the real old school, who had driven and worked horses all his life. We bought the plough, two sets of harrows, a steerage horse-hoe, a garden cultivator, a muck cart, several oil lamps, stone bottles, a bundle of hand tools and I don't know what-all besides—for five pounds.

Pinto didn't think much of the plough. But there is one thing about getting a pony in front of a plough—he can't run away with you. You can anchor him. Sally had to lead Pinto while I ploughed, or I led him while she ploughed, and our good friend the owner of the water-mill came up one day when we were struggling at it (and it was a struggle) and took over, and showed us how to adjust the plough, and by and by both Sally and I, and Pinto, got broken in to it, and now although I am quite certain we would not win a ploughing competition, we can at least turn over the ground.

Not that we need to plough very much with our new style of farming. The pigs do it for us. This year, on The Hill, when the pigs had finished rooting out the artichokes, we simply made Pinto lug a section of heavy harrow about a few times, then light harrowed it, then drilled it with the Jalo hand-drill. The ground was never ploughed. And I have never seen a better bit of beet.

We used the plough last year though for ploughing in our potatoes, and ploughing them out again; and that saved an enormous amount of labour. We followed the ploughing-out with the pigs, and they rooted up every tuber which we did not find, so nothing was wasted.

Pinto is marvellous for pulling either a "hoop hoe" (which is just what it says), or a garden cultivator, up and down between the rows of row crops. This saves us days of hoeing. We still have to whip through with the hand-hoe to get the weeds in the rows, but not having to hand-hoe between the rows is a great help. Pinto pulls these things very fast—at a fast walk in fact, one has a job to keep up with him. He is wonderful for pulling the light harrows over the grassland, to spread the manure and pull out the rubbish. We make him pull a garden roller, for rolling land for kale and the like.

But now that we have no motor-car we use him for very much more than a plough horse.

Yesterday we took a load of green pots up to our kiln in the village to fire. We had to balance them on a big drawer placed in the governess-cart, and a ticklish old job it was. But, *in'sh'allah*! not one of them broke.

Today an old friend walked some way to come and see us, and we put Pinto in the cart and drove him back to the village where he had left his car, and showed him a bit of the countryside. Tomorrow evening I shall drive five miles away to see a man who may sell us some weaner pigs. I shall be there and back in two hours, and have done my business and downed a couple of pints into the bargain.

Of course we are lucky in living in a remote part of the country, where the roads are comparatively free from horseless carriages. Also in living in a fairly flat country: hills slow a horse up terribly.

As to the cost: I suppose we bought horse and equipage and implements for just inside the hundred pounds. For food—we have been feeding Pinto bought hay lately, for the reasons that I gave in preceding chapters: having ploughed up half our own grassland to reseed it, we have not enough grass of our own. We have retreated the better to jump. He gets five shillings worth of hay a week, besides of course some grass.

A rough-bred pony such as Pinto will live, and work quite hard, on grass alone, winter and summer. The thing to guard against is letting him have too much grass in the summer, for if you do he will not only get fat and lazy but he will get laminitis. He will quite happily live out of doors winter and summer. Again I hear all the lady-humanitarians phoning for the police —but how do they think wild ponies live on Exmoor, or the Black Mountain, or the Fells, or the Scottish moors? Why don't they start a campaign for getting all the reindeer into houses? A pony, if he is used to it, will keep healthier out of doors, winter and summer, than he will in.

But if you want to work a horse or a pony *hard*—trot long distances on the road, ride to hounds, plough all day: you must feed him more than grass, and it is better if you stable him. You are making him act in an unnatural manner, and therefore you must treat him unnaturally. You must feed him hay, strictly limit his intake of grass, and, according to how hard he works, give him oats.

Pinto, in this year of grace, gets stabled at night, with a small amount of good hay, and for part of the day he is pegged out on the lawn, or on other odd bits of grassland which we want nibbling down but can't trust the cow there. On some days he gets worked a little, although never very much. Our cultivations never go on for more than an hour or so—or maybe an afternoon of light harrowing at the most. We are lucky in having some very nice small boys who come from the village, being for some unaccountable reason immune from the telly, and ride Pinto, and in return for this pleasure will work him for me in front of the harrows, or help me to lead him when I want to row-cultivate.

A nice thing about driving about in a horse and cart is the tremendous interest taken in you by the older country people. We have never lacked good *advice*. The first time I drove to a favourite pub of mine, which is just seven miles away, I got an almost royal reception. When we at last got chucked out, about seven men, all of them fairly full of beer, insisted on harnessing the pony up for me, and putting him in the shafts. They had all worked with horses, and it reminded them of the days when life wasn't quite so complicated.

We have had this interest about all our anachronistic back-to-the-land activities.

When we first got a cow old cowmen would come down to look at her, and give us advice (which was better than every book in the world), and give us any help we needed. We never go into the village without inquiries being made as to the welfare of our stock. When we got pigs we were loaded with tales of "when *we* always kep' a pig in the back garden—and very nice that woor too 'bor!" Instead of being foreigners, as we might well have remained in this particular part of Suffolk for the next twenty years, we are accepted. We are doing what many of the old inhabitants once did do—and would now *like* to do. There is just that old *spiritus mundi* that's stopping them.

The other day an old friend called to see us—a Traveller. When we had last seen him he and his wife had been living in a horse-drawn canvas-topped van—we had been sleeping in the back of a Dormobile. This time when we met him we were driving a pony and cart—*he* was driving a beautiful converted Bedford ambulance, with plush curtains in the windows, a silver greyhound on the radiator cap, chrome plate all over it. We both laughed and asked each other who had come up—and who down. And neither of us was quite sure.

And we don't only drive Pinto to the pub and back.

Last April Sally and I wanted a holiday, and the girl who had been living with us for some months helping, looking after the children, was able to get her mother and father down to stay at the Broom for a month. We railed Pinto and the cart to Margate, of all places, and drove him from there to Luccombe, in Somerset, camping out every night in a tent. We drove him, on nothing but grass eked out with an occasional handful of oats, three hundred and forty miles in twenty-one days. Then we railed him back from Minehead.

Try doing that with a garden tractor.

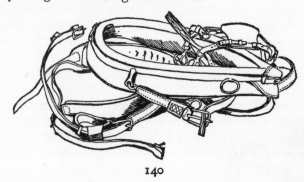

12

Up to Now

A difficulty about writing a book of this kind is that the story is changing all the time that you are writing it. What I wrote three chapters ago is already out of date. As I am coming to the end of my saga now, though, I will try to bring it as far as now, Tuesday the 22nd of November 1960.

We went for yet another pony and cart trip through East Anglia, being away for all the month of September, and getting as far as Bury Saint Edmunds in West Suffolk, and Wells and Norwich in Norfolk. It rained most of the time.

We had left the Broom in good order, had left Brownie with some black and white ladies in a farm by the sea (the equivalent to her of a Butlin's holiday camp I suppose), Esau with a boy named Dickie who comes to see us from the village a lot, and Dickie looked after our ducks, hens, and geese. Pinto, of course, we took with us.

We drove back once in a borrowed car, and spent an hour pulling weeds out of the fodder beet on The Hill, and another hour picking and salting down runner beans of which there was an enormous crop. We filled a six-gallon crock with them. We did not see the Broom again until we drove Pinto back to it in early October.

The jungle had returned.

Goose Bit, The Hill, those parts of the front garden which were not lawn, were masses of weeds. White bryony, fat hen, nightshade, nettles both annual and perennial, thistles, spear grass—everything else you can think of.

Up to Now

The quarter of an acre of artichokes which we had planted with so much labour in the nearest end of Star Goose (the field) were twelve-feet high though and had smothered every weed in their area. It was pitch dark beneath them, and under there nothing could live. The fodder beet on the hill were clean enough (goodness knows they had been hoed and weeded enough) and promised to be a heavy crop. Most of the garden crops in Goose Bit had already been harvested and the land was now five-feet high with weeds. Spear grass had recolonized all the land so laboriously cleared of it in the previous three and a half years.

The reason for this was of course the rain. The summer of 1959 was the driest ever recorded in England: that of 1960 the wettest. We were not alone in suffering from this invasion of weeds. Everyone else in the area was the same. Even people who had quite small gardens and had been there to care for them had been beaten by the revolution of the weeds. It was a full-scale counter-attack.

We worried about it at first, but then decided to forget about the weeds, attend to the harvesting of such crops as needed it, and deal with the weed menace later on in the winter when the exuberance of the enemy had at least been tempered by the frosts.

The worst hit was the little vineyard. The vines straggled about in a jungle of rank annual weeds, and grass had completely recolonized the area. The reason for this was that as I had not wired and tied the vines as I should have done it had been impossible properly to clean the ground between them before we had gone on the pony and cart trip, and so the weeds had had a head start. The vineyard is still like this, as I write, but shortly I shall attack it with a vengeance: wiring and pruning the vines first so as to get them out of the way, then clearing the ground with the mattock (laborious but very effective) then cultivating up and down between the rows fairly often with the horse.

The potatoes were the first job. They were a sparse crop—the incessant wet had not apparently favoured them. But they

143

were sound and clean, and the tubers were a good size, and I began to lift them by hand.

The reason for reverting to hand-lifting was because the potatoes had been planted when we had been away in the spring (on our first pony and cart trip) by a friend. He had planted them well enough, but for some reason for which he had had no explanation had planted the rows across the long, narrow, side of Goose Bit, instead of along it, and it was too short a distance for the pony to work with the plough. Hence a job that should have taken me a morning took me weeks. But hand-lifting had this advantage: I really did get out a lot of spear grass and bindweed roots.

As for the crop—I get ten good barrow-loads, which I daresay is getting on for a ton. And that of clean potatoes—there is about five hundredweight more of seed and pig potatoes. Not enough to fatten the pigs on this year, but enough to feed us until potatoes come again.

The fodder beet I am still lifting.

I pull a few every day and top them, and every day I put the tops that I cut off a week before into an opened sack and carry them on my back to the cow. Her milk went up as soon as she started eating them. She is now getting a mere double handful of crushed oats at each milking, with a handful of groundnut cake in it, as much fodder beet tops as she can eat, a few mangels, a little hay, and what she can scrounge in the end of Star Goose and in the wood. On this diet she is doing very well. She is in calf—due, I should think, in about next April.

As soon as we got back we bought three pigs. Large-White-Landrace cross, two gilts and a hog, bought at twelve-weeks old from a smallholder neighbour for six pounds each. They are running on the artichokes now, and have already grubbed up about a quarter of them. I am feeding them fodder-beet tops and also a few fodder beet, and as many mangels as they can eat. With this they get about one pound each a day of R. and W. Paul's "Four to One"—a highly concentrated high protein mixture, and about the same amount of Paul's "No. 2 Pig Meal", and also, I should not forget, all the scraps from the house and all the dishwater. They are absolutely thriving. They live in a terrible ramshackle sty which originally had straw-stuffed wire-netting walls but they have pulled all the straw out. They nest down, however, in a great mass of old reeds, which have been pulled off our roof.

For the thatchers are here.

Several weeks ago our young thatcher friend Jeremy, and his wife Rosemary, and their two small boys Philip and Paul, and Jeremy'. young apprentice Ted, all arrived in a van, and started thatching our roof.

They were terribly held up, firstly by the weather for the rain still goes on unceasingly—having broken every previous year's record for rain this year keeps on breaking its own record—and then by the reed, some of which was too short, rotten, and unsuitable. We had a row with the suppliers, and eventually persuaded them to replace some of it; but the thatching was held up for over a week.

We have learnt a lot about this thatching business. As thatch would be in every way the best material to use for a man who decided to build his own cottage or house on his own bit of land and become a peasant I will retail a little of what we have learnt.

In the first place there are three main sorts of material used for thatching in England, and they are as different as chalk from cheese.

The material which has been used most in the east of England and the Midlands, and which has given thatch its bad name, is known to thatchers as "long straw". This is simply wheat straw, which has passed through a threshing drum, which is piled in a great heap in the garden, drenched with buckets and buckets of water, pulled out in handfuls from under the heap, tied in bundles, and put on the roof. It is tatty after a very few years, is finished at ten or twelve, looks like a large dung-hill even when it is new, becomes infested with birds and rats and mice, and easily catches on fire. It is what most people think of when they hear the word "thatch".

The other material used in East Anglia is so-called "Norfolk reed". I say so-called because it grows in many other parts of the country too.

This is the perfect thatching material. It is exceedingly quick to put on, lasts from seventy to a hundred years, resists rodents and birds, is almost impossible to set on fire, and looks delightful. It has one disadvantage: it is in short supply. It is cut from reed beds which are flooded, some by fresh water and some by brack water. Cutting it is hard work, and must be done between about Christmas and the end of March. Later than that the new reed begins to grow, and also pheasants start to pair and landlords do not like the countryside disturbed. On the Broads, where most of it comes from, men go out in boats to cut it and carry it home, and work with a hand scythe of a special design, often in winter blizzards. It is tough hard work, and not many men are willing to do it. So it is scarce, and it is expensive. Enough to do the Broom—back only (the front and sides do not need doing, having been done only twenty years ago) cost us eighty-five pounds.

But there is an acceptable alternative, which *could* be cheap.

In the west of England, where Jeremy served his time as a thatcher, a material called *wheat reed* is used.

This may sound to the uninitiated just like "long straw" for it is the same material in fact: the straw of the wheat plant. But it is completely different from "long straw", and is, in fact, much more like Norfolk reed. It is the straw of specially selected varieties of wheat (the old-English varieties like Yeoman and Little Joss), grown on land which has been heavily dunged (artificials will produce a heavy crop of grain but weak straw), cut a fortnight before the grain is properly ripe, allowed to dry in the stook, then allowed to mature in the rick, and then—and here is the most important thing—threshed in such a way as not to damage the straw.

Of course this means that the straw must not pass through a threshing drum. There are two ways of threshing it without letting this happen: one is by means of a "comber", which fits on to the top of a threshing drum and holds the straw while allowing just the ears to reach the drum and then withdraws the straw, combs it, and ties it in bundles. The other is to thresh it by hand, by bashing it over a barrel so as to knock the grain out of the ears. It must then be pulled through the teeth of a big comb to straighten it and remove all the "flag", or leaf, and then it is carefully bundled and tied.

Roofs of this material have never been made in the eastern counties, where Norfolk reed and long straw have been the rule. In the west of England such roofs last thirty years—but roofs of Norfolk reed do not last much more than that there anyway! So the assumption can be made that "wheat reed", put into roofs in the dry eastern counties, would last as long as Norfolk reed does—i.e. nearly a man's lifetime.

And it *could* be a lot cheaper than Norfolk reed. At present it is, in the east of England, unobtainable. It is the sort of thing a smallholder could produce to advantage for himself. For he could grow the right varieties of wheat, on well-dunged land, and thresh it out by hand himself. How nice to grow the roof of one's own house.

Thatch, unfortunately, has come to be associated with dear old maiden ladies who have "twee" cottages built for themselves in twee little country villages, with thatch coming down all round to make them look like tea-cosies. There is one monstrous bungalow at the seaside with a vast thatched roof, and iron spiders' webs over the tiny windows, and you have to keep the electric light on all day inside it if you want to be able to see your hand in front of your eyes. It is this sort of thing that has given thatch a bad name.

In fact, for a man building a new house in the country, thatch has enormous advantages.

It is (contrary to what one is told by so-called "experts") exceedingly cheap. The thatching itself, if done with Norfolk reed, might spoil the look of a couple of hundred pounds or more, but consider the timbering of the roof. Thatch requires much lighter timber than any other form of roof and—a very big advantage—it can be laid on green unseasoned timber, and furthermore on unsawn timber. You could go out into a wood and cut down fairly straight poles, bark them, and put them straight into the roof. The timber will season perfectly in the roof, for the thatch keeps it dry and ventilated, and at a perfectly even temperature. If you put a thermometer under a thatched roof you will find that the temperature hardly varies winter or summer. Timber under thatch seems to keep good for ever.

Further, thatch halves your fuel bills.

Churchwardens of thatched churches in Norfolk and Suffolk make this claim at any rate, and anyone can feel for himself the difference between walking into a thatched church during mid-week and walking into the clammy ecclesiastical chill of a church with any other form of roof. Certainly our house at the Broom keeps snug and warm and dry with very little in the way of firing.

Further—in the countryside thatch looks good. I do not mean "twee" thatch—ye olde Englishe thatch—that looks terrible and there is far too much of it. But honest thatch just put there because it is the cheapest and best form of roof. Nothing looks better, nor blends in better with any background. It is the natural country roofing material in all but rocky countries.

And lastly, a man might, with a little learning, grow and make his own thatched roof. Mind you—it would take him a long time, and it might not look perfect. But, at a pinch, I believe he could do it.

During the thatching of our roof I had to make considerable inquiries into the thatching industry in East Anglia, for when we found that the reed supplied us in the first place was inferior I had to look around for an alternative source of supply. Luckily, in the end, this was not necessary, for the original suppliers replaced the worst of it.

But what I found made me think that a disturbing development is taking place in the thatching industry.

There are growing up big thatching firms, employing numbers of men. These firms operate over a very wide area of country—some of them claim to undertake work anywhere in England in fact—and therefore the local idiosyncrasies of thatch —the regional differences that make thatch so interesting—

these differences will disappear. It is all part of the drive in the world today to make *every* place look like *every* other place. It is deplorable. Furthermore the old local thatchers were good and independent men, and most of them charged only enough to make a living and honest wage.

One firm of big thatchers in Norfolk quoted me £50 for three hundred bundles of reeds delivered to my house! They knew, as well as I did, that the biggest price they could with honesty have asked, was half of this sum. An honest individual reed cutter on the Broads eventually offered reeds to me at a shilling a bundle. These companies and large firms are getting a stranglehold on the reed supplies. They are gradually forcing the small thatchers out of business. Then of course—it is "we can give you a job in our firm". The independent man becomes a wage slave. These big firms depend on *ignorance*. The users of thatch know nothing about it. They think that, because a firm is big, it will be more reliable. They think because the big firms charge more their work must be better. In most cases this is simply not so. But it takes you twenty or thirty years to find this out.

The hope of thatch in East Anglia, I should say, would be to develop "wheat reed". This would break the monopoly of the reed suppliers, and bring good *reed* thatch down to a reasonable price again.

"Long straw" thatch is something that should not be considered at all. What on earth is the use of putting on a roof that will have to be done again in twelve years' time? One can see how long straw thatching came about.

Every farm, in the days before the combine harvester and the baling machine, had plenty of good wheat straw. Every farm had a man on it, or at least had a man on call in the parish, who could thatch hay stacks and corn ricks. If a farmer built a cottage for a man it was cheap and easy for him to have that cottage thatched with his own straw and by his own thatcher. Labour was so cheap as to be almost a negligible financial consideration. What if he had to put on another coat of thatch in twelve years? It cost practically nothing.

But now with the minimum agricultural wage as high as it is "long straw" thatching is economically out of the question.

The answer is for smallholders and small farmers to grow wheat or rye and comb the straw for the production of "wheat reed". This would then knock the price of "Norfolk" reed down to where it ought to be, and would ensure a big enough production of high quality thatching material to thatch all the roofs requiring it in the country. And people would again learn that thatch is an excellent and economical roofing material.

It is a little strange that our Government in this country finances a thing called the Rural Industries Bureau which employs "thatching officers" who go about the country trying to encourage people to use thatch, and at the same time the Government will give a grant of 33⅓ per cent of the cost to anybody in the country who rips thatch off a roof and replaces it with tiles. If I had tiled the Broom I would have got this grant. Because I caused it to be reroofed with thatch I had to pay the cost all out of my own pocket. How illogical can a government be?

One very pleasant outcome of the visit of Jeremy and his family here is that they have decided to stay in East Anglia. They drove over to the Breckland country and saw the agent of a big estate there, and he offered them the tenancy of a farmhouse, in a remote place by a mere, with five acres of land and outbuildings attached to it. They are going to settle there, Jeremy will practise his craft, and they will run the holding and try to be at least partly self-supporting. There are, God knows, plenty of roofs for them to thatch. East Anglia is full of houses and cottages with neglected thatched roofs.

Soon after we got back in October we bought an old builder's van for five pounds. A retired builder at a nearby village said he would sell it to me—if I helped him get it out. For, for the last ten years, it has lain in a shed behind a great permanent fence which he had put up to keep both boys and cats out. We had to knock down the fence first, then harness Pinto on to the van, and drag it out. It is a most elegant and beautiful vehicle: with varnished panelled sides, raking backwards, fine springing, four "patent" wooden wheels, and you sit high up to drive it. Pinto is far too small for it and we must one day look for a bigger horse.

The need for this was illustrated by what amounted almost to a gift of several tons of mangels.

The crop in Pony Marsh this year—that is the long narrow arable field next to the Broom which is farmed by our landlord (alas—I wish it was farmed by us but one must not be greedy) was mangels, or what are called about here "cattle beet". Michael pulled most of them and got them off with a trailer behind two tractors. The time came, however, when the land got too wet and boggy even for this and he had his work cut out salvaging the trailer and the tractors. He told me the other day, therefore, that if I cared to harvest the remaining six or seven tons and get them out with my horse I could have them at a nominal price.

Accordingly Sally, Jeremy, and myself went one evening and pulled them all, topped a few, and then took Pinto in, dragging the four-wheeler van.

Alas. As soon as we were properly in the mud Pinto decided that he could go no farther. Urged—he not only went backwards—and reared up—but he lay down. It took us all our time to get him to drag that van, still empty, out of there.

There was only one thing to do, and we are doing it day by day as I write. When I have finished writing this chapter I shall have lunch, and then go out into Pony Marsh. I shall top mangels into two bag baskets that I have there, hoist them up on a yoke, and carry them back to the clamp that I am making in Star Goose. (The yoke, by the way, was one of the very few things we came here with from the boat. We bought it from a turner in Boston, Lincs, and used to use it for carrying jerry-cans of fuel oil or fresh water aboard.)

I suppose that it would be considered pretty "un-modern" to carry mangel-wurzles about with a yoke nowadays. I don't care —I am not going to see all that good stock-food go to waste. I am going to carry them, and we are going to try to buy half a

dozen sheep to help eat them, for already we have enough
fodder beet of our own growing for the cow.

So here we are, snug under our new thatched roof. We face
the winter not unprepared, although we are short of certain
things. There have been five adults and four children and a
baby living here for five weeks, with more most week-ends; and
such a force must make inroads into the storeroom. We only
have half a ham left and no bacon. There is still, however,
some salt pork and there are a few tins of roast pork left. Jam
will not last us out, for we were away during the jam-making
season and the black currants let us down and so did the gooseberries. Green tomato pickle and chutney we have in plenty,
and also pickled shallots. Onions might have lasted just our
own family, but could not feed the multitude. They will, I fear,
give out about Christmas time. We have no bottled ripe tomatoes this year for the crop was a failure, and no dried sweet
corn. Plenty of haricot beans though. Three hundred salt
herring. Five fattening geese to kill, and plenty of ducks and
chickens. We will kill a porker before Christmas and two
baconers after it, so next year we should not run short of pig
meat. Green vegetables are better this year than before but—
alas—we did not have time this year to plant celery. That is a
sore loss. Apples, we have enough stored to last half-way

through the winter. Wine we are beginning to see building up to a decent stock, and this Christmas will not be a teetotal one, thank God. Brownie we will have to dry off in February or March and will then probably buy a second cow. Next year, and I hope in every year to come, there will be enough grass and clover for both summer and winter feeding for two cows.

So we do not face starvation. What we do face though, with all those weeds, is a lot of hard work.

13

Our Foreign Trade

I am a word monger, and very little else. I serve up words in whatever form I can get paid for them—like this, over the ether, in magazines—I even gave a lecture to a rotary club meeting once but it was all a big mistake.

Sally, though, is an artist and a craftsman. She has a natural feeling for form, for materials, for fitness, for line and for colour. She will turn her hand to anything within her strength, and she is not above calling for mine on occasion.

She is primarily a potter, and a first-class one. I have heard people say that she is one of the best decorators of pottery in the country. Certainly her pottery has this quality: it is pleasing to people of every stage of sophistication. She does a great trade in beer mugs amongst local farm workers, and yet mugs with the same designs on, or the same sort of designs, she can sell to the most sophisticated and "advanced" shops in London.

She is also an illustrator, and if she put the same effort into illustrating as she does into cheese making could be in the top class.

It might be said, in fact it often has been said, that it is deplorable that somebody who has these talents should waste her time doing things that anybody else could do, like making cheeses and bottling fruit.

This may be so. But the thing is with Sally—if she wants to make a cheese she will make a cheese, and nothing on earth—certainly not her husband—will stop her. The Father Art

Our Foreign Trade

Editor of all Art Editors could come on his bended knees and offer her the moon and the stars, but she will not let that milk go sour before she puts the rennet in, not for nobody.

I have tried, in vain, to make her take a financial view of things. She just does not think financially. "If you", I have said, "would do those illustrations for the such and such you would get twenty guineas. You can buy an awful lot of cheese for twenty guineas."

"But I *like* making cheese," she says. And that is that. The whole financial argument crashes to the ground.

And it may be that she is quite right. In any case, we never argue seriously about it, because I think exactly the same way.

It is through listening always to the financial argument that so many people in the world lead such boring lives. You may be able to buy cheese for four shillings a pound, but you cannot buy Sally's cheese for four pounds a pound. It is not for sale.

But it is obvious that we must do some trade with the rest of the world, and so we set aside a part of each day to making things that the rest of the world will want. It is important, though, that the goods that we offer should be very good, and that the goods that we buy in exchange should be good too. And there we come into very deep water.

I used to think that an old petrol tin was as good for carrying water in as an earthenware pot. One day I read something written by Tagore, in which he touched on this very comparison. He said—yes—an old petrol tin is as good for carrying water as a *chatti*, or one of the beautiful pots that Indian women carry on their heads, except for one thing: the petrol tin is mean. It is grudging. Because it just serves the utilitarian purpose—*and no more*. It carries the water all right. So does the *chatti*. But the *chatti* is delightful to look at, delightful to feel and to touch, pleasant to have around. Every time you look at it you think of the love and care with which it was made, by the hands of a human being. Every time you look at the petrol tin you think of a huge, ugly, clanking, dirty machine, mindlessly slamming out ugly objects. For no machine-made artifact can be beautiful. Beauty in artifacts can only be put there by the hands of the craftsman, and no machine will ever be built that can replace these. Machines might one day be made which will appreciate the beauty of articles made by other machines. People can only be truly pleased by articles made by other people.

As far as possible we buy only things that have been made by people, and not by machines. I do not mean necessarily by the bare hands of people—hands can be magnified by tools and machines—but the hands must be there. Cloth woven on a loom—by a man—is fine. Cloth woven on a loom—by an automatic device—is dull. It is grudging, like the empty petrol tin. It only serves the one purpose.

But we have to buy, occasionally, the grudging things. The only way to treat the twentieth century is, not to ignore it, but not to let oneself be overruled by it. Not to drive a car just because it is "modern". But to be prepared to drive a car if it will serve some really good purpose—some purpose that has nothing to do with some intellectual and probably fallacious conception of "progress". And even then it is generally better to go in a sailing boat, or a pony trap.

Sally uses an electric kiln for firing her pots. She decorates them mostly with under-glaze colours, and fires up to 1,150 degrees. Because she uses colour and fine line and draughtsmanship she needs to fire within very narrow temperature limits, and an electric kiln is the best tool for this. But she does not let herself be ruled by her electric kiln. She does not say: "If I taught a lot of giggling girls to come and decorate my pots with stencils of my designs, and installed an automatic machine for slamming out pots to my shapes, and installed a continuous high-production kiln, I would make very much more money than I am making now." She would no doubt make very much more money. She would be "turning out" very many more pots. She would be able to sell them a little cheaper perhaps. A lot more people could have Sally pots in their homes. But they would be little better than petrol tins. And instead of being that fine and happy thing—an artist and a craftsman—she would become that miserable and unhappy thing—a money-grubber.

Our Foreign Trade

And all we could do with the grudging things that her machines made would be to exchange them for the grudging things that other people's machines made.

A friend came and tried to build her a wood-fired kiln here once, and the beginnings of it, four courses of fire bricks high, stand there still, a monument to a splendid failure. One day we may complete it, and then fire pots, much rougher and less decorated ones than the ones that Sally makes now, to a lower temperature, but more cheaply. We could make for our own use, and for sale, ordinary utilitarian things, like Tagore's *chattis*, at prices which could complete with mass-produced rubbish. Meanwhile we have enough else to do.

So Sally pots when she can, and her pots sell very readily at a fair price. At this time she is too busy potting babies to be able to do much other potting, so that sector of our export trade is in temporary decline. If we could get electricity at the Broom potting would be a lot easier: it is extremely difficult when you have to fire in the village, and slog a mile and a half to turn the kiln off, perhaps at four o'clock in the morning.

As the kiln is in the pub I generally manage to make turning-off time for the kiln coincide with turning-out time at the pub. But this, though pleasant, is apt to be expensive.

So for the main part our balance of trade is maintained by my word-mongering. And here another sort of balance has to be struck. Am I to do a great deal of writing, broadcasting, recording, and all the rest of it—and allow our peasant holding to go backwards? Or am I to work the holding at the expense of the other? For six months now we have not had a car. I could earn more money if we had a car: but what would the car cost me? For every time we engage in any trade with the industrial world we are gearing ourselves up with the industrial economy, and it becomes harder to live by our own peasant economy. We are beginning to be more and more convinced that it is better to stay quietly at home, only do such writing as we really feel is worth doing for its own sake as well as for the sake of the money we get from it, and keep our trade with the industrial world at a minimum. Electricity would be another gearing-up with industrialism. It might be worth it—it might not. I am not talking in terms of money-worth—but in another kind of worth. It would be nice to be able to switch the light on, and have an automatic electric pump to fill the tank on the roof. But what price would we have to pay—in independence? When we bought the Aga—we were binding ourselves for ever to have to import coke. If we had made a big open hearth we could have remained self-supporting in fuel. There will always be enough firewood here, if somebody has the energy to go and get it. Now that we have imported all the capital equipment that a peasant needs (or most of it) we could live here very comfortably on a hundred pounds a year, for that would cover our rent, rates, flour, seed, and oddments, and also clothes, for we could be even more self-supporting than we are now—if we had the time to give to it. We could very easily grow our own wheat, barley and oats, and possibly rye.

We should get eighteen hundredweight of corn off an acre. This is certainly more than we at present have to buy for ourselves and our stock. And an acre of our five acres under corn every year would fit in nicely with our economy.

There is indeed another possibility with regard to this corn growing.

Any farming reader will by now have said to himself: "Yes—but if he grows this corn—how is he going to thresh it?"

For we obviously could not get a threshing drum to come all the way down here to thresh such a small quantity of corn. Well—we could thresh it by hand—over a barrel. And this would make the straw qualify as "wheat reed" for thatching, and our friend Jeremy would buy it from us at £25 a ton, and as we should grow a ton on our acre that would pay our rent.

There is coming about a great shortage of "Norfolk reed" in this country. The coypus are doing great damage to the beds.

Also many of the sources of supply are coming into the hands of company thatchers, who—when they have created enough of a monopoly—will no doubt hold the consumer up to ransom. Before I managed to get the suppliers of my reed to change some I tried to buy three hundred bundles to finish this roof and one large firm quoted me fifty pounds for them (see page 149). They, as I did, knew that the proper price was fifteen pounds—not fifty. They knew that I was in difficulties over obtaining a supply, and were simply holding me up to ransom. But there is no doubt—there is going to be an increasing demand for good thatching material. Thatch is still the cheapest and best roof you can have—if it is done with reed, either "Norfolk" or "wheat", and not with "long straw". I do not see why the smallholder should not take advantage of this fact, growing his own wheat or rye, and make the hand-threshing of it not just a painful necessity but a big advantage. For by hand-threshing it he can get twenty-five pounds a ton for his straw—instead of probably nothing at all, for straw nowadays is a drug on the market.

Sally and I have been lucky in this matter of being able to live the Robinson Crusoe existence and at the same time carry on a limited trade with the world. Sally was already a potter, I already a writer. But I often think what I would do were I a young man, starting out in life, and with cranky ambitions to be self-supporting on five acres.

Well—I would learn a trade. Not writing, which is dicey in the extreme, and cannot be learnt in any case. But some honest trade.

My friend Jeremy (who is only twenty-one) has solved the problem beautifully. His father was a thatcher, he has served his time under him, is now a master thatcher himself, and has an apprentice—a boy of eighteen. He will have an assured very good living for the rest of his life. There is a great shortage of good thatchers. These "dying trades" are only dying because young men think they are. The *spiritus mundi* is against them. In fact there has never been a greater demand for thatchers, blacksmiths, farriers, saddlers (a miserable mass-produced saddle costs thirty guineas), carpenters, masons, cabinet-makers, any maker of fine hand-made articles. This demand will increase, not decrease.

Supposing a young man apprenticed himself, only for a year say, to a cooper. The trade of coopery is dead? Try buying a four-and-a-half gallon cask for home-made wine at a reasonable price! A man could learn to make casks, go and live in the country, turn out good-looking small wine casks, advertise them in selected national weeklies, rail them all over the country to the growing legion of amateur wine makers—and he would not "make a fortune"—he would make something infinitely better—a good and honest living. He would make an honest living, in his own time, in his own shed, and have time left over to run a smallholding and feed himself. Such a man would be a happy man. He would have complete security, because he would *know* that he could always earn a living. For he would not *need* to overcharge, or continually "increase his production", or mechanize, or call in "work study experts". He could feed himself and his family anyway.

Hurdle-making. Bob Ward's Carr—the wood next to the Broom—has five acres (at a guess) of mixed alder and ash coppice. If I were a hurdle-maker and not a writer I would buy that off my landlord, split the best of the ash up for hurdles, saw the rest up and hawk it round as firewood. It would not be spoiling the wood—it would be farming it, for the coppice would grow up again and soon produce more material. How pleasantly thus could I supply our modest needs!

Basket making. Price the next waste-paper basket you see in a shop. Nothing is easier than to establish a few acres of osier beds, and no use of land is more profitable. Rush-weaving. My neighbour learnt how to do this, and now has a factory in a nearby town which employs a giggle of girls turning the stuff out: table mats, rush baskets, rush carpets (everlasting but terribly expensive), "display material", many other things. And the demand for his products is insatiable. Ordinary cloth weaving is, surprisingly enough, most profitable, as you can find out by visiting a few hand weavers. What do you have to pay for continental sausages in this country? There alone is a living.

There are plenty of ways, besides potting and word-mongering, by which a peasant-craftsman can balance his export-import trade in England today. There is only one proviso—he must be a master of whatever trade he has. It is the bad studio-potters who go broke in such large numbers. "Hand made" should not be synonymous with "roughly made". The hand-made article should be far better than the machine-made equivalent. The craftsman should master his craft. This need not take the seven years of the old-fashioned apprenticeship. The old-time apprentice spent the first six years of his seven making tea.

As far as possible we like to trade with other cranks. Not only because this helps them, but because it decreases our dependence on the industrial world. Direct barter is a very good idea. Let the inland revenue try to get their experts around that.

We give some thought to this export problem though. We have considered other strings to our bow. A little commercial pig-keeping, or egg producing, might not be a bad thing, and we may come round to it. A friend gave us a very old but very good printing press, and we do all our own printing—letter heads, Christmas cards, wine labels, etc. The title page of this book shows our wine label. We plan to make Christmas cards in limited editions commercially, and also possibly small books for small children. Why not? Another form of export trade, in which we can engage with enjoyment. As peasants we can consider these things. If I worked from nine to five in an office or a factory I would not have the spirit left to consider anything.

As it is, I believe that our foreign trade is healthy. We started with nothing except an overdraft. We now have a little money and nearly all the capital equipment that a peasant needs to live well (and as far as food goes we live better than anybody else I know in this country), and we have bought a lot of experience. We now do not need to earn so much "foreign exchange". We can concentrate more on the internal development of our own holding. We can, therefore, afford to stop making goods "for export" excepting goods which we really believe are good. In other words—no more "hack" writing. But the corollary of this is—probably—no more motor-cars.

You cannot have it both ways. But we do not intend to be slaves to our muck heap and our mud patch. We have just come back from a month's trip through the country with Pinto and the cart, the second this year. We arranged for a neighbour to come and throw some corn to the fowls, and Brownie cow we boarded out on a farm with some other ladies. All was well when we got back—except that the incessant rain of this year had caused such an explosion of weeds in the garden that it will take us the winter to clean the ground again. We have not given up the idea of foreign travel. We might at any time pack our livestock off to market, perhaps let friends come and live here for a year, put the dug land down to grass and let our landlord graze it while we are away. It is a firm base to come back to. The fertility that we have built up here will still be here when we get back.

Sane people think that we are "cranks" to live the way we do. Of course, being sane, they are right. We are rip-roaring cranks. And what fun it is too.

We often feel like saying, with the lunatic who was looking over the wall of the asylum watching the strange doings of the people in the street: "Come inside!"

14

Thirteen Years After

Well, what have we learned?

What has altered since I wrote *The Fat of the Land* thirteen years ago; what have we discovered that we should have done and didn't do, or should not have done and did do?

The first big change is that now we are not alone. When we found ourselves becoming self-sufficient in food at the Broom we were probably the only family in England living in this way. Now there are hundreds doing it—and tens of thousands who would like to. In America the thing has become an epidemic and is causing concern to the authorities. American "Communiteers" and self-supporters run their own magazines and newspapers, have at least one school for training themselves, and number themselves now in thousands in every state of the Union. Of course nearly all hippies have as part of their philosophy the ideal of becoming self-sufficient. Few of them have achieved it as yet because they cannot tear themselves away from their guitars long enough. But many of them have had a try.

Other changes are: the soaring price of land, the drying-up of the empty cottages in the countryside that I wrote of in the book, the drying-up of cheap horse-drawn and other old implements (they are bought up by antique dealers now and hung on pub walls) and the even greater intrusion of the State into every corner of private life.

Thirteen Years After

We are not at the Broom any more. Wishing to own land of our own we went to Pembrokeshire, nine years ago, and bought a small farm. To the question of "how did we pay for it?" the answer is we never have. We bought the whole thing on a mortgage and a bank overdraft. Not only did we not have *one penny* when we signed the contract to buy it—we actually had an overdraft already. Which goes to show that most things are possible if you've got enough neck.

The farm is now, thank God for us, worth at least five times what we *didn't* pay for it. I thank God from a selfish point of view only: from the point of view of humanity I think it is a disaster. It is now quite impossible for all but the very rich to own land at all in this country. I would like to start a society, the object of which would be to find out *who owns England* and then to make the ordinary Englishman take an interest in the ownership of his country. Is the present structure of ownership of land in this country the best possible for ourselves, for our posterity, and, most important of all, for the land? When people write to me now asking my advice on how they can get their equivalent of the Broom I have to write back and say that, in all probability, they can't. If they work hard all their lives, and live to be a hundred, they still won't be able to buy any land, nor would they be allowed to build a house on it if they could. Maybe up in the Pennines somewhere or in Ireland or the West of Scotland. . . . Even here in Pembrokeshire land prices have shot right over the top: it is years since any local farmer's son has been able to get a farm around us: businessmen come from England and bid the prices up far beyond their reach.

Well, we got in just in time. We bought our seventy acres for £4,250 of borrowed money, and it had on it a more or less derelict two-bedroomed house. Not being able to afford to pay someone to move us we borrowed yet more money and bought a 7-ton cattle-truck and did it ourselves, selling the truck afterwards for a little less than we paid for it. We made three voyages in it, carrying all we possessed: furniture, implements, animals, children and the charming girl who happened to be sharing our lives at the time, her wages paid for out of Sally's pot money. In the last voyage we carried most of the animals: one very big horse, three cows, twelve geese, some sitting on eggs, twenty ducks, very many hens, a dog, and the cat locked in the meat safe. We stopped for diesel oil in the middle of the night, and a sleepy pump attendant came out to serve us and just at that moment, awakened by the cessation of movement, every one of the animals and birds woke up. The horse began to whinny and kick, the cows to bellow, the hens to cackle, the dog to bark, the cat to yowl, the geese to honk, and the twenty ducks put their heads out of the ventilation slot right at the top and began to quack in chorus. "Christ!" said the pump attendant. "Christ!" And he went pale. If he had been a Catholic he would have crossed himself. When we got to our farm and released the cat from the meat safe we found it covered in broken goose eggs and goose manure. It let out a horrid shriek, and lit off for the mountains.

In Wales life changed for us completely. For one thing we found ourselves in the midst of a still-peasant society. Our neighbours had not yet all given up brewing their own beer, killing their own pigs, and living largely from their own holdings. This fact made life immediately pleasanter for us: we no longer felt that we were freaks. I'll never forget our first hay-making. We had met nobody at that time, had hired a contractor to cut a dozen acres of grass, had made it by hand, and hired another contractor to come and bale it. Sally and I were busy carrying the bales to the barn in the back of a 7-cwt. van—a most laborious task! Suddenly we heard the sound of singing, and of tractor engines. We saw two tractors drawing trailers come into our field, and a dozen singing Welshmen, and, without speaking to us, they loaded all our hay up, carried it to our barn, and stacked it. They then produced big stoneware jars of home brewed beer, and we all sat on the bales in the hay barn and drank it, and I learned two things—one was the necessity for brewing one's own beer, the other was the value of neighbourly co-operation: something that has practically died out in the East of England.

But as for self-sufficiency: it goes on now much harder than it did before. Everything we did in Suffolk we started to do here, except the growing of crops that would grow there but won't grow here very well. And several things we didn't do in Suffolk we do here. We have crashed the corn barrier for example. Here we grow oats, barley and wheat; we have got the little Canadian mill that Jack Blake sold us for thirty bob going and we grind our own bread flour. We brew our own beer, and will very soon be malting our own barley to do it with. And we are probably the only people in West Wales who grow hops.

It is delightful to live among peasants. My neighbours might not take it as a compliment to be called this but I mean it as a compliment. They are still—the smaller farmers anyway—human. They are not right bowed down yet in worship of the Golden Calf. They have not yet become entirely "agri-businessmen"—the thing that all our agricultural economists are for ever urging us to be. They still have time to help each other, to farm for the good of their land as well as their pocket, to drink and to sing and to be happy. The country is delightful, the land and the climate difficult but endlessly interesting; we are near the sea and have sea fish galore; we have forest and tons of good firewood; we rear and kill all our own beef, mutton and pig meat, are never short of vegetables, and are probably as self-supporting as one family could be on its own.

But the thing that I have learnt is that it was a mistake to try to live like this alone. Sally would not agree with me here—she has always been against us having anything to do with other people. If I ever mention the idea of getting somebody on the farm to help us she says: "Oh no—we don't want to start some bloody community!" And so we have tried to do too much, have worked too hard, have forgotten what it is to sit and listen to music in the evening, or read something just for pleasure, or to engage for hours in amusing or interesting conversation. We can never both leave the house together. The children are now bigger, and very helpful and very much on our side, but even so—there are not enough of us. If a number of families could get together, buy a farm, build each a house on it, and then co-operate in a flexible sort of way—"A" keeps cows and keeps us all in dairy products, "B" grows corn and keeps us in flour, animal food and malt, "D" keeps pigs and poultry: something like that—then I think they could lead very good lives indeed. In the United States there are now thousands of communities of every kind of make-up, from the hugger-mugger community where everybody hops in and out of bed with each other to the sort of loosely knit association that I have described. How successful they are in being nice places to live in I have no idea, but I do know that many of them have survived for a long time now, and that their numbers are increasing. The price of land and the planning laws make all such experiments impossible in this country: if you could buy the land you couldn't get permission to build on it. Our planning laws are completely wrong for our country I believe, and should be completely revised. They seldom seem to stop some "developer" from committing the most appalling despoliation of the countryside if he is going to make money out of it. But they hamper at every turn the man who wants to establish a home for himself, not in a town. They are designed for the rapidly *decreasing* number of enormously rich farmers, (decreasing because as farms get larger farmers get fewer) and the city dweller who likes to drive out, at a weekend, and see miles of empty and half-farmed countryside and think to himself: "What lovely unspoiled country!" before he buries his nose in the *News of the World*, which is what he is really dying to do.

But this is a democracy, and if enough people wanted to change things, things would be changed. But the Englishman is a *city* man—never was there a more completely urban civilization than ours. He doesn't know who owns the countryside and he doesn't care. He is completely indifferent about it. He imagines his food as nearly all coming from abroad anyway, and the country to him is just empty space between his town and the next.

There is one criticism that we self-supporters must answer though, if we wish ever to have any chance of being taken seriously. And that is the allegation that the self-sufficient peasant is not making the best use of his land. Can we justify, in other words, the occupation of, say, five acres of land by one family wishing to feed itself off it in a world where the population is outstripping the acres?

Unfortunately the people who advance this criticism are townspeople who just do not know anything about farming at all, and therefore it is very difficult to argue with them. In a world where land is short surely the only criterion about whether land is being used well or no is—how much food is it producing per unit of its surface! When we went to the Broom the five-acre plot that we had there was very rough and poor grazing indeed. It was just a tiny and unregarded corner of a big estate, and if Michael's cowman had forgotten to open the gate into it for a year or two it wouldn't have made the slightest difference to Michael's economy. By the time we had finished with it that land was producing a very high yield of very high quality food, both animal and vegetable. You may say: "but it wasn't feeding anybody but you!" Well, *somebody*—some land— would have had to feed us had we lived in Birmingham. And as it was, besides feeding us, there was always, willy-nilly, a big surplus for sale to other people. Here, in Wales, we have drained the marshes, fenced the whole farm where no fences were before, cleared away the encroaching scrub, planted an orchard, planted hundreds of forest trees, and turned a derelict place into a productive one. If there were enough *people* on it— enough *hands*—I believe that our seventy acres could produce a dozen times as much *food* as it did before. The big landowner— the large scale agri-businessman—does not care about a high production of food per acre. What he is interested in is profit, and he can achieve this by specialization (always the enemy of good husbandry), mechanization, and the lavish use of chemicals. His chief expense will always be labour—and labour he must cut out at any cost. There is a man I know of who farms ten thousand acres with three men (and the use of some contractors). Of course he can only grow one crop— barley, and of course his production *per acre* is very low and his consumption of imported fertilizer very high. He burns all his straw, puts no humus on the land (he boasts there isn't a four-footed animal on it—but I have seen a hare) and he knows perfectly well his land will suffer in the end. He doesn't care—it will see him out. He is already a millionaire several times over. He is the prime example of that darling of the agricultural economist—the successful agri-businessman.

Cut that land (exhausted as it is) up into a thousand plots of ten acres each, give each plot to a family trained to use it, and within ten years the production coming from it would be enormous. It would make a really massive contribution to the balance of payments problem. The motorist with his *News of the World* wouldn't have the satisfaction of looking over a vast treeless, hedgeless prairie of indifferent barley—but he could get out of his car for a change and wander through a seemingly huge area of diverse countryside, orchards, young tree plantations, a myriad small plots of land growing a multiplicity of different crops, farm animals galore, and hundreds of happy and healthy children. Even the agricultural economist has convinced himself of one thing. He will tell you (if he is any good) that land farmed in big units has a low production of food per acre but a high production of food per man-hour, and that land farmed in small units has the opposite—a very poor production per man-hour but a high production per acre. He will then say that in a competitive world we must go for high production per man-hour and not per acre. I would disagree with him.

As for the personal aspect—would I advise anybody to try to become a self-supporter?—well I wouldn't advise anybody to do anything. After all—it is so easy to get that job in the air-conditioned office, and catch the eight-thirty—and get very well paid for doing very little at all. Why should a man take the hard way?

I only know it suits *me*. It is the only way I could conceive of living. From the health point of view of course there is just no argument about it at all. We have reared four children who are quite monotonously healthy; I don't know the name of our doctor; when we all troop into the dentist for our yearly check-up he makes a great joke of it because he has never yet found anything wrong with any of us (except when Kate broke a tooth falling off a horse). It is years since any of us got a tooth filled and the incidence of dental caries in our family over the years is—nil. At well on in my fifties I have not so far felt the slightest diminution of my energy or physical fitness. There is nothing I could do at twenty-five that I cannot do better now. I can still (and often do) walk the thirty-five miles in a day over rough country and enjoy the last mile as much as the first. Only last summer I sailed an open boat several hundred miles along the coast, sleeping rough on the bottom boards. I'm not boasting—I am just producing evidence that the self-supporting life is good for you.

I am sure we have been right in repudiating the rubbish and gadgetry of industrial society. I am sure it is wrong for people to have to live in housing estates and work in huge factories to produce such rubbish. I don't think the human animal has been evolved by natural selection to live happily like that—any more than the domestic fowl has been bred by natural selection to be happy in a small wire cage.

As for the charge: "Aren't you an escapist—aren't you being a bit selfish?" I would answer that by asking if one of the Gadarene swine would have been open to the charge of selfishness if he had declined to go over the cliff with the others? Escapist yes—well then, all right, I am an escapist. I hope I shall go on escaping. But in our eighteen years of "crankery" we have never had a penny off "The Nash", "The Labour" or "The Health" (except for a couple of weeks or so when I had a knee operation—made necessary by dancing a fandango with a plump lady at four o'clock in the morning after drinking too much home brew); we have always been able somehow or other to "stamp our cards", pay our rates and taxes; we have made some land highly productive that wasn't productive at all before; Sally continues to work full time as a potter and has a constant waiting list of people wanting to buy her pots; I am a productive writer. If anybody accuses us of living non-productive lives I would like to take him up on it.

So I would assert that anybody who *wants* to be a self-supporter should be allowed to be one, if he can show first

hat he knows how to do it. Maybe he should have to work
'or an experienced man first for a few years, or qualify himself
n some other way.

If a man says: "Give me my share of my country provided
that I can look after it in a sound and husband-like manner"
I think it should be made possible for him to have it. Make
him pay for it by all means—make him work for it—make it
hard to get—but make it possible for him to get it. Nowadays
it is getting less and less possible.

I know that governments, and those dismal men called
"economists", are all trying to "phase out" the small farmer
and drive him into the cities to release more land for big
farmers. I think this is wrong. The governments are misguided
and the "economists" have been given the wrong brief. The
economists have been told to make the farmer richer. Well
there is one sure way of making a farmer richer (short of
increasing the price of food) and that is to give him a bigger
farm. Now, the only way to give farmers bigger farms (short
of creating more land) is to reduce the number of farmers. The
only way to do this is to take the land away from existing
farmers and drive them into the cities. This suits the governments because it increases the size of the pool of exploitable
labour for industry and makes their countries "greater" by
hardening their currency and producing more exportable goods.

Well, this may lead to "richness" and "greatness" but it
won't lead to happiness, or to health either—health either for
people or land. The health of human beings is important but
the health of the land is the most important thing in the world;
without it *all* life will fail on this planet. I am quite sure that
the health of the land is not improved by enlarging the size of
farms. The *richness* of the few farmers left is increased of course,
you don't have to be an "economist" to see that. The bigger
the farm the richer the farmer. But the health and well-being
of humanity as a whole, the beauty and real utility of the
countryside, and above all *the health of the land*—all these things
are diminished and not improved. Also the economist has
never even *heard* of that new phenomenon (a very old phen-

omenon really but coming to life again): the man who farms a piece of land to produce his food but also works at some non-agricultural profession or trade. Now this man, if he works hard and well at his trade or profession—*and* at his piece of land, is a very valuable member of the community, is a happy man, rears a happy and healthy family, and he does good to his piece of land. He increases the production from it, and leaves it better than he found it. He is a better citizen than any "economist" or politician in the history of the world.

To help such people, Sally and I have written a book, the fruit of our eighteen years of direct experience at being self-supporting (and a good many more years on my side at least in farming, and observing farming, in a dozen or a score of countries around the globe—I've lost count) and also of a pretty exhaustive reading of the literature on the many arts and sciences bearing on the subject in England, and we've called this book: *Self-Sufficiency: The Science and Art of Producing and Preserving your own Food.* This is not a gardening book, nor a cookery book, but it deals with the whole process of starting with a piece of bare land, and ending up with a regular supply of all the kinds of foodstuffs that a family of people could want or need in a temperate climate. There is no kind of food or drink that can be produced in a temperate climate that you cannot produce yourself on your own bit of land, if you have one, excluding fish and salt, and these too you can produce for yourself if you live near the sea. In *Self Sufficiency* we have tried to tell you how to do it. Except for a very few items we have done it ourselves.

An argument I am always hearing when I talk of the right of people to have their own piece of land is: "But most people in England don't *want* a piece of land!"

Well, if they don't want it they needn't have it. All the more for people who do.

I am reminded of a neighbour of mine in Pembrokeshire who came out of the door of the pub with a glass of beer in his hand, to accost the Salvation Army meeting that had started in the street outside. The Salvationists were not singing, out listening to one of their number preaching.

"*Sing*—you bastards—*sing*!" shouted my neighbour.

"I will have you know Sir," said one of them, "I am not a bastard!"

"Well you needn't sing!" said my neighbour.

The townsman who doesn't *want* his piece of his country needn't have it. That's the answer to that. As for the ones who *do* want it—well, this is a democracy. They should set about contriving to get it.

Index

Accountancy, 43
Artichokes, globe, 56
  root, 80, 81, 92 et seq.
Artificial manures, 51
Asparagus, 52

Brassicas, *see* Cabbage tribe
Bacon curing, 104 et seq.
Beans, broad, 55
  runner, french and haricot,
    56
  runner, preserving, 107
Beauty, 123
Beet, cattle and fodder, 92, 95
Bottling, 107 et seq.
Brawn, 101
Bread, 34, 98
Butchering, 77 et seq., 99, 101
Butter, 45

Cabbage, red, 56
  tribe, 52
Canning, 101 et seq.
Carrots, 52, 55
Celery, 57
Cheese, 45, 106
Chickens, 28, 30, 31
Cloches, 36

Comfrey, 94
Corn, 32, 98, 158
Cow, 41 et seq.
Cucumbers, 56
Cultivation, 36, 86 et seq., 92 et
    seq.

Dairy, 64
Decorating (house), 59 et seq.
Ducks, 26 et seq.

Fishing, 129 et seq.
Food preserving, 99 et seq.
Fruit, 37 et seq., 50. *See also*
    Soft fruit
Fuel, 69 et seq.
Furniture, 13, 39, 61

Geese, 26 et seq.

Hay, 44, 88
Herrings, 113
Horse, 132 et seq.
Hospitality, 136
House, 17, 65 et seq., 72

Kale, 51
Kitchen, 63

Labour costs, 43
Larder, 63, 65
Laundry, 64
Leeks, 52
Lettuce, 52

Mangolds, *see* Beet
Manure, 51
Marrow tribe, 56
Milk, 44
Milking, 42
Moles, 58

Onions, 51, 53, 55

Parsnips, 52
Peas, 55
Pigs, 73 et seq.
Pigsties, 80
Planting, 36
Potatoes, 53 et seq.
Pottery, 156, 157
Progress, 124
Poultry, *see* Chickens
Pumpkins, *see* Marrow tribe

Rabbits, 31
Rhubarb, 52
Rubbish, 68

Soft fruit, 38, 50
Spinach, 52
Stove, cooking, 61 et seq.
Swedes, 54
Sweet corn, 55
    preserving, 107

Thatch, 66, 145 et seq.
Tomatoes, 57, 72
    preserving, 107
Tools, 114 et seq.
Trade, 29, 154 et seq.

Vegetables, 50 et seq.
Vegetarianism, 32
Vineyard, 94

Water, 25, 66 et seq.
Wheat, *see* Corn
Wild food, 108, 125
Wine, 109 et seq.